G. W. Kroek

*

The Magi
At Christmas

A Winter Love Story

Erica House

BALTIMORE   AMSTERDAM

First printing

ISBN: 0-9659308-7-4

PUBLISHED BY ERICA HOUSE BOOK PUBLISHERS
Baltimore, Maryland   Amsterdam, the Netherlands

Printed in the United States of America

For Elaine --

a promise kept

Acknowledgements

I would like to thank all those who played a part in bringing *Magi* into being, especially my daughter Cammeron, my greatest fan, who read the earliest draft and believed from the beginning that this was "the book."

Also, Morgan and Christine Higgins who read it early on when I wasn't sure whether it was "very bad" or "very good," but pretty sure it was one or the other. Friend and fellow writer Sid Krome has been a champion of my work for almost as long as we have known one another, but his belief that *Magi* would become a Christmas classic spurred me during the frustrating hunt for a publisher.

A special thanks to Karen Shumaker who has been a faithful reader and sounding board for almost as long as we have been friends. Thanks to colleague Marjorie Burnham for the first check of my German, and to my good friend Hartmut Klose in Seevetal, Germany for the finetuning. And my heartfelt gratitude to Janice Jones, probably the most beautiful pregnant lady I have ever known, who shared with me not only resources on pregnancy and delivery but so much about her own experience of the process, especially her hopes and fears.

Don and Jeri Bone have been the best of friends and have believed in me since our university days, and it thrills me that they feel as much joy in this publication as I do. And finally, Wim Meiners, my publisher, who from the first reading "loved it" and believed in the story as much as I did, enough to take on an unknown writer and help make the magic real.

1

Strange, but as he sat there on the verge of fulfilling a dream, he felt even more dispirited than he had in months. None of it was working out as he had planned and hoped, as nothing really had since the divorce. An undertow of despair seemed to draw him steadily toward some swirling, shadowy vortex that as yet had no name. He tried to pull himself free of such currents with the thought that he was at least doing it, at least doing something, rather than drifting as he had for months -- Christ, at least he could be honest with himself, couldn't he -- for years now.

The Lufthansa business class was certainly comfortable enough with lots of room for his long legs. He thought of those early years when he had been building up the business, all that travel by coach and cheap charters, the sardine-like confinement, the seemingly endless hours from LAX to Paris, to Frankfurt, to Rome. By the time there were flights to Sydney, Santiago and Johannesburg, though, he no longer had to make them, or when he did, he always flew business or first class.

The flight seemed full. Even though he had made countless trips to Europe, this was his first during the Christmas season, and he had had no idea that the plane would be so crowded. Looking around, he noticed that the only vacant seat in business seemed to be the window seat beside him, and he certainly hoped it would remain so. If there was one thing he didn't need, it was company, and he especially didn't feel like making small talk all the way to Frankfurt.

"Let's make a final head-count, Lilly," one attractive flight attendant said to another.

Maybe his luck would hold. Maybe this flight he would even be able to sleep, something he seldom could do, but for some reason he felt very tired, almost lethargic. He closed his eyes and drifted, waded aimlessly in the shoals, through the clutter and refuse of his life, the raw-edged debris now tumbled, buffed and smoothed by the ebb and flow of his constant combing, but still sharp-edged enough to wound a tender foot, or an unsuspecting hand. But his luck did not hold.

"Here you are, Miss. You're very fortunate, you know. This is the very last seat on the flight," he heard the flight attendant say before opening his eyes.

Oh Christ! She was young and . . . and . . . he didn't know quite what. He watched her struggle to get a large, blue-denim duffle bag in the overhead compartment. Her hair was cut short, bobbed, with even shorter bangs, black with strange purple streaks and highlights. A silver ring pierced her right nostril and another smaller one her left eyebrow, and a series of dark-stoned studs curved around the edge of her right ear as well. From the other, a series of graduated black beads hung on a slender silver thread, so heavy the whole pulled down and distorted her earlobe. It was only then that he noticed her pregnancy.

"Here," he blurted too loudly, jumping up, upset with himself for noticing the wrong things. "Let me help with that."

"Thank you. I can't quite reach that high." She gave him a faint smile that faded as quickly as it had come.

Her black lipstick stood out against the pallor of her skin. It had to be powdered, right? Nobody's skin was that pale. Dark liner set off her eyes, but it wasn't the liner that drew him, rather the eyes themselves, a lavender gray like he had never seen before. The total package was somehow unsettling,

8

he thought, and then he became aware of her standing patiently waiting for him to put her bag in the overhead. Even as he made room for the blue denim duffle beside his own carry-on, he grumbled to himself. Of all the people in business, he would be the one to get stuck with her. Nose ring. Eyebrow ring. Probably a silver-balled stud through her tongue and safety pins piercing her nipples, surely some kind of ring or stud in her navel, maybe even a pussy ring. He had heard of such things. She was just one more broken, splintered piece of his collapsing Christmas fantasy.

"Sorry," she said in a soft voice, without even the hint of a studded lisp.

"No problem." He moved aside so that she could take the window seat.

"Maybe . . . maybe you want to sit there," she said. "I have to pee a lot, you know." Her slim fingers ran down over the swell of her stomach, and then she gave a quick shrug of her frail shoulders, moving like small wings beneath the black of the sheath that fell to her ankles, the only break the rotund belly that protruded like a soccer ball. He didn't know which, but either her thinness exaggerated her pregnancy, or vice versa. Finally he noticed the clunky combat boots that had once been so popular. "I really don't want to be a pain in the ass." She stood waiting for him to decide.

"Sure, why not?" He did not like window seats, always asked for an aisle, but he remembered when his wife had been pregnant. He really didn't need to be disturbed every time she had to get up and trot off to the bathroom.

"Thanks." She sat down and buckled the seat belt over her surprisingly slim thighs, and beneath her belly's protrusion. Another faint smile. "This is nice."

Nice! he said to himself. Great! "Better than back there," he said to her with a tilt of his his head, wishing that that was exactly where she was -- where she belonged?

"I'm really lucky, I guess. I was on stand-by. Cheap seat."

Your luck, my misfortune, almost tripped off his tongue. He was afraid she was going to be a chatter-box, but to his surprise, those were the last words she uttered for a long while. She looked around the compartment, at the passengers, the flight attendants, seeming to study every detail. But he noticed that as soon as the plane began to move backward out of the bay, she gripped the arms of the seat so hard that the tendons stood out in her small, fine-boned hands. Even though she wore no ring, at least not on her finger, he supposed she was some GI's wife flying to be with her husband for Christmas.

The girl paid studious attention as the flight attendant led them through the safety procedures, the laminated folder open on her lap, turning her head to look for EXIT signs, looking for the string of lights that would direct her down the aisle in case the power failed. Her right hand even moved beneath the seat to check where the life preserver could be found in case of a water landing. He decided not to frighten her further and tell her just what their chances would be if such a landing became necessary. From time to time she looked across at him, but he tried to avoid meeting such glances, avoiding those black-lined lavender eyes. Better to ignore than engage and chatter.

He thought of his own daughter, pleased that even though everything in her life was not as he might wish it, at least she didn't dress like . . . like this girl. Amanda was twenty-four, almost twenty-five, and taught aerobics between boyfriends. She had had no desire whatsoever to attend college, and she spent most of her time at the beach, sure that her sunscreen and youth would protect her from skin cancer. The girl who sat beside him could at least do with a little of his daughter's deep tan. Amanda would spend Christmas with her boyfriend in San Francisco -- one large piece of his plan that had gone awry early on.

As the huge jet engines revved for take off, the girl beside him gripped the armrests even tighter, and then the plane was hurtling down the run-way faster than even he imagined it could, always the same, and he never ceased to be surprised, rushing toward the moment when the wheels lifted off the concrete runway and he was caught between earth and sky, his stomach reluctant to come along.

And then the fingers of her right hand clamped around his forearm, tightening as the plane climbed sharply and then banked just as steeply out over the ocean. The strength of her grip surprised him, but just as quickly, as the plane began to level off, her hand sprang away.

"Oh, God, I'm so sorry . . . I just. . . I . . . I don't . . ."

"That's okay," he said, finding her vulnerability somehow reassuring. "First flight?"

She nodded. "First everything, almost."

Well, not *everything*, he thought to himself as he looked down at the swollen evidence of at least one adventure.

"It's almost an E Ticket, I suppose, if you've never done it before."

She smiled at him and said, "Sorry about the arm."

"Nothing broken," he returned, moving his hand around for her, aware that neither her voice nor her demeanor matched her looks.

Later, when the plane had reached its cruising altitude, the flight attendant came by. "What would you like to drink?" she asked the girl coolly. "It will be a while before we serve dinner."

"Do you have decaffeinated Coke?" the girl asked.

"Yes."

"Good, that's what I'll have then."

"And you, Sir?" she said, smiling.

"Do you still have that wonderful Wehlener Sonnenuhr Kabinett?" he asked hopefully.

"Yes we do, Sir. A good choice," she said, her smile broadening.

It *was* a good choice, he knew. If there was one thing that he did know, it was wine. He had to. And when the girl's Coke and his glass of Mosel arrived, he was pleased that it was every bit as good as he had remembered. So good that he felt compelled to recommend it to the strange creature that sat beside him sipping her soda.

"Do you fly a lot?" the girl asked.

"Not as much as I used to, but yes, now and then. Why?"

"You knew about that wine."

"Oh, yes, it's been a while, though, and I didn't know if they would still be carrying it. I was afraid that something this good might have been gone by now. You really should have a glass sometime during the flight. You don't generally get such a good wine on an airline. It's really excellent -- of course, that assumes you enjoy Mosel," he said, holding up the glass and tilting it so that the overhead reading light set off the pale gold.

"I'm sure it is, but my baby doesn't drink alcohol, smoke or do drugs," she said without a smile.

How could he have been so thoughtless? "Good for you," he said, trying to wiggle free from his stupid *faux pas*. Maybe his first impressions of the girl had been wrong.

It seemed that the older he got, the more aware he became that nothing was ever simple. He sipped his wine and questioned his journey. Had his plan deflated, sagged into some flaccid mistake? Was he just being stubborn? He could be, he knew, but he had dreamed for so long of spending Christmas in Germany, and now he was doing it, even if he was doing it without his family, doing it all alone, probably doing it all wrong.

The flight had gone smoothly and for him quickly. He had even slept for several hours, a real rarity. Thanks to her suggestion, the girl's frequent trips to the bathroom hadn't disturbed him in the least, and she hadn't tried to engage him in conversation even once. Most of the flight that he had been aware of her, she had been listening to her own Walkman, eyes closed, fingers laced and hands resting gently upon her unborn baby, or reading from a tattered paperback.

When the announcement came that the flight was beginning its descent into Frankfurt, a pain in itself, no direct flight to Munich in winter, he began to feel bad that he had been such a poor fellow traveler. He supposed that his own disappointments might have influenced his reaction to the girl, so in the remaining few minutes he tried to make up for it.

"Are you meeting your husband?" he asked, breaking hours of silence.

"Ah . . . well . . . ah . . . kind of," she responded, obviously startled by his abrupt question. "I'm really going on to Munich."

"Spending Christmas together?"

"Well . . . I guess so."

Strange answer, he thought.

"And you?" she asked in a soft voice.

"Me? No, I don't have a husband," he said, trying to make a small joke, but she didn't smile.

"I meant family." She turned away from him.

"No . . . no . . . yes, I do have a family, but they are back in the States. I had hoped that we would all be together here for Christmas, but it hasn't worked out that way. I'll be spending Christmas alone."

"That's too bad," she said, looking back at him, and then added almost inaudibly, "At least you have a family."

So softly, in fact, that he wasn't even sure that it was addressed to him. Since he didn't know how to respond, he kept his mouth shut. After the plane had landed without incident and finally lurched to a stop, she got up and tried to reach the overhead latch, but he jumped up.

"Here, I'll get that for you." He opened the compartment, lifted out her large duffle and sat it on the seat, and then he took down his own. "Everything okay?" he asked her, for she looked as though she were about to cry.

"Yes . . . no . . . I don't know. I've never been anywhere before. I don't know what to do. I don't speak the language."

"No problem, really. Lots of people speak English, especially in the airport. Just go through immigration control, show your passport, then go pick up your luggage. They'll tell us what carousel our luggage will be on. Anyway, there are signs above the carousels with the flight numbers. Get your bags, follow the green lines--you don't have anything to declare, right? And if you have any . . . you know, controlled substances or whatever, just leave it on the plane. They are really hard on you here."

"I told you, my baby doesn't do drugs, and neither do I."

"Okay, it was just a little friendly advice." One stupid mistake after another, he realized.

"I'm just a little concerned about making my connecting flight and all." She chewed gently at the corner of her dark mouth.

Great! Would he never be free of this strange creature. "Don't worry about it. I'm going on to Munich myself, so I'll make sure you get to the right gate, okay?"

"Thank you. I'd really appreciate it." Again, she chewed, taking the corner of her lower lip between her teeth.

When they began to debark, he offered to carry her bag, but she refused; however, she did stay close to him as they passed through passport control, and then down toward the luggage claim. She hung off to one side, her bag at her feet, as he waited for his luggage. When it finally arrived, large, well-

14

used but sturdy with a pull-out handle and wide-set wheels, he noticed that she had nothing but the duffel.

"Don't you have any luggage?"

She shook her bobbed head and knocked the sole of one booted foot against the other nervously.

Well, maybe if she were meeting her husband in Munich, she didn't need much. Who was he to second guess anyone? After clearing customs, and checking his suitcase back in, they still had about an hour to wile away before the flight to Munich. He decided to deposit his unlikely charge at the gate and then find a nice quiet place, or at least a relatively quiet place, to have a cup of strong German coffee, just one of the things he loved about the country.

"Here you are, Miss." He looked at his watch and said, "It will probably be about half an hour or so before they board. Okay?"

"It's Heilman, Jennifer Heilman, Jenny. And thank you again. You've been really nice."

"Don't mention it, Miss Heilman." He hadn't been going to give her his name, but there was something sad beneath all that makeup and paraphernalia, something extremely fragile behind those strange lavender eyes. "My name's Erik Leiden. Perhaps I'll see you on the flight," he said, already turning to begin his search for that somewhat quiet cafe and that cup of coffee that beckoned.

As he sipped his coffee, he began to wonder if he shouldn't just go back to the Lufthansa counter and book the earliest flight home. He knew that there was one in the afternoon. He had taken it many times. This whole trip was just a bit crazy, wasn't it? His dream of being here at Christmas had included his family, but now, wifeless, children scattered to the winds back in California, did his pilgrimage make any sense?

Still, he was here, and he did love Germany. Furthermore, he certainly knew the *Drei Könige* Hotel in the Bavarian

Forest, its owners, the Holzmans, old acquaintances whom he hadn't seen in some years. No, he would just make the best of it, come what might. Christmas had always been a magical time for him, ever since he had been a child. Who knew, maybe he would discover a bit of magic in the *Drei Könige*. At worst, he would have lots of good cooking and wonderful beer and wine. Anyway, Christmas at the *Drei Könige* couldn't be any worse than Christmas alone in his Santa Monica condo, could it?

When he got back to the gate, the first call to board had just been given, and the flight to Munich boarded promptly, lifted off on time, and less than an hour later, landed flawlessly and then howled down the runway, stirring up great clouds of swirling snow. Out the window he could see mounds of plowed white dozed up along the route. It all looked pretty fresh to him. One final opportunity to reconsider returning home, he thought as the lumbering jet taxied toward its gate.

2

He had never been in Munich's new airport before, and it seemed unfinished and barn-like. All that space must have been planned, but it struck him only as strange, and everything coldly geometric. All airports being pretty much the same, he looked for the sign with the black silhouette of an auto and the German word *Autovermietung*. His pre-paid car would be waiting. One last chance to change his mind, he thought. He would have to cancel it if he returned to the States. Anyway, maybe the *Lebkuchen*, *Pfeffernüsse*, *Stollen* and *Glühwein* would be enough. Hell, maybe he could even get to Nürnberg for the *Christkindlesmarkt*, that most famous of Christmas markets. Yes, he would just ride it out, and play it as it came.

Just as he picked up the signs for the car rentals, he saw the girl standing with two young police officers or soldiers --he could never tell which patrolled the airports with their fresh faces and submachine guns. They were all three engaged in animated conversation, and the girl seemed on the verge of tears. Jesus, had she been arrested? All that about her baby not doing drugs a bunch of malarkey? Maybe she wasn't even pregnant! Wouldn't that be something, a belly full of drugs or some other illegal contraband. He was tempted to pass by, but if she were in some kind of trouble, she would need somebody, and there wasn't anyone around who looked like a husband.

"Hello there," he said. "Everything okay, Miss . . . ?" He couldn't remember the name she had given him.

"Oh, thank heavens, Mr. Leiden," she said, brightening, not only recognizing him, but remembering *his* name. She reached out and took one sleeve of his sport coat and drew him into the small circle. "This man was on the flight with me," she said to the young officers.

"My name is Erik Leiden, USA," he said to them. "What's the problem?" he asked the girl, but before she could answer, the uniformed female, looking every bit as young as the girl, spoke up.

"Miss Heilman says that all her money was stolen from her purse," the officer said in perfect English and gestured toward the bag which hung from the young girl's shoulder. "Just a flap, not even a clasp," she added with a frown.

"Yes, I was coming down the escalators when the person in front of me stumbled and fell back against me. I almost fell backward too, but this man behind caught me. They were both real nice, the one apologized, and the other made sure I was okay. But I think they're the ones who stole my money, because I went from there straight to the *Geldwechselstube*, or however you say it, and when I tried to get D-Marks, I discovered all my money was gone. Almost five hundred dollars! All the money I had!"

"Did they get anything else? Passport? Credit cards?" he asked.

"No, I still had my passport in my hand for some reason, and I don't have any credit cards."

The female officer cleared her throat. "We have taken down all the information, Sir, and we will do what we can, but there is not much we can do." She shook her head, and looked genuinely concerned. "We will circulate their description," she continued, looking at the girl, "but even if they are caught, which is not likely," she waved around the milling throng in the airport, "I promise you, they will have no American dollars with them."

"Can't you do something?" she pleaded with him, tugging at his sleeve.

"I would if I could, Miss Heilman, but they're right, I'm afraid. A sadder but wiser girl, huh?"

"That may be, but now what am I supposed to do." She was angry, but the anger came in tears and a blue vein that pulsed along the right side of her slender throat.

"Your husband hasn't arrived yet?" he asked her.

"There isn't any husband," she blurted out between sobs.

"But I thought you were . . ."

"I told you there isn't any. No one is coming. I'm all alone." She looked down as one booted foot moved against the other.

"Oh," was all he could say. What the hell was he supposed to do now? "Okay, okay, you still have your passport, right?"

She nodded.

"All you have to do is get to the American Consulate here in Munich. I've never had the need to test the theory, but as I understand it, they will see to it that you get home if you don't have the means to get there yourself." Good solution. Got her out of his hair as well. How was it that she kept cropping up, anyway?

He unclasped his own travel bag and took out his wallet. He pulled out two twenty D-Mark notes and a ten. "Here, this should get you to the Consulate by taxi with some to spare, and they should be able to get you home."

She pushed his hand away with an angry shove. It came away wet and warm from her tears. "I don't want your money, and I didn't come all this way just to turn around and go home," she said, almost stomping one foot, but easing it down at the last moment. "I just want . . . to find my . . . baby's father," she said, ushering in a new bout of sobbing.

"Okay, okay," he said, putting his arm awkwardly around her thin shoulders, suddenly aware that the two officers had melted away, and he was all alone with her. He didn't blame them. There was really nothing they could do. Why hadn't he himself just kept walking? "Come on, let's sit over here," he said, motioning toward an empty bench.

"I'm sorry I'm causing all this fuss. You've been real nice to help me."

"Well, in all honesty, I haven't helped you, and I don't know that I can, but why don't you tell me what's going on -- I mean, if you feel you can."

She began crying again, the darker streaks left behind by her tears confirming at least the ghostly powdered complexion. He gave her his handkerchief, and she dabbed at her eyes and blew her nose tentatively, the white linen coming away damp with dark smudges.

"I'm not married, Mr. Leiden. Never was."

"But you said that you were meeting your --"

"No, not really."

"So there's no one coming to meet you at all?"

"No, no one."

"I guess I don't understand, then. What are you doing here?"

"I'm here to find my baby's father."

"So you know where he is then?"

"Well, I have an address. But I'm not sure."

"Not sure?"

"No. I've written lots of letters, but they've all come back. They have some kind of stamp on them, but it's in German. Even the woman at the post office didn't know what it meant."

"Probably no longer at that address -- or maybe even an incorrect address."

She just shrugged those frail, birdlike shoulders.

"You mean to tell me you came all this way without even knowing for sure if this guy even lives here?"

"It's all I had. He told me he was stationed in Regensburg, Germany, and he left me this address." She dug in her purse and pulled out a slip of worn, pink paper that had been folded and unfolded so many times that the two halves barely hung together. She handed it to him.

James Castle

Habsburgerstr. 1414

82135 Regensburg

Germany

"You say he's in the military?"

"Yes. Army."

"You know, single men don't usually live off post, and this certainly isn't a post address. You're sure about this?"

"He wrote it out. It's all I have."

"Miss Heilman, you are either the gutsiest girl I've ever met, or the craziest. I'm not sure which. You really expect to find this guy?"

"I have to try, Mr. Leiden. It's all I have to go on. My baby needs a father. A family. I just didn't know what else to do. I'm due next month. I'm not even supposed to be flying, this far along and all. They told me at the free clinic where I go, but I just had to take the chance. I didn't even know if they would let me on the plane, but I don't look eight month, I guess."

"Well, I sure can't advise you."

"I don't know what to do. When I left home, I felt like I was doing the right thing, but now I just don't know. I feel so lost, Mr. Leiden."

"Listen, I'm probably just as crazy as you are, but I'll tell you what . . . I should really make you take this money and go to the Consulate, but I somehow don't think you'd do that. Right?" He smiled at her and she managed a weak smile in return. "So what I'm going to do is offer you a ride to Regensburg. I was on my way to pick up my rental car, so you can tag along if you like. I'm heading for the Bavarian Forest, a little town called Bodenmais. I'm going to spend Christmas there, but I guess Regensburg isn't really that far away from where I turn off the Autobahn, maybe fifty miles or so northwest, if I remember. On the Autobahn, really not that far, I imagine. What do you say?"

"Oh, thank you, thank you, thank you." She took his hand and placed it against her cheek. "I don't know what I would have done without you."

"Okay, Miss Heilman. I'll get you to Regensburg. If I have time, we'll try to find the address, and if he's there, great. If not, I'll have to drop you off at the *Rathaus* or something, and then you're on your own, fair enough?"

"Yeah, but what's a rat house?" she asked with a strange frown.

"Not rat house, *Rathaus*. It's the German word for courthouse, municipal building, whatever."

She smiled at him and said, "Okay, I'll take the ride," she said, holding out her small hand to shake on it. "But how come you are being so nice to me? I know it isn't for sex," she said patting her tummy.

"You are blunt, aren't you, Miss Heilman? And you're right. You see, I have a daughter not much older than you, and I would sure want someone to help her if she were far away from home and in trouble," the old-fashioned meaning of the word dawning on him only after the fact.

"She is sure lucky to have a dad like you."

Right, he thought to himself. That's why I'm here and she's going to be in San Francisco, but this poor creature didn't need to know anything about that.

"Mr. Leiden, could you call me Jenny? I feel funny when you call me Miss Heilman."

"Okay, then you must call me Erik."

After he had turned in his voucher at the rental agency, signed all the proper documents, and had been given the keys, they made their way to the parking structure, rode up to the fourth floor and found the steel gray Mercedes. After winding down the tight, spiraling ramp, they pulled out of the building and onto the road leading to the Autobahn. She reached over and touched his arm.

"Thank you again, Mr. Leiden. This is just so nice of you. I know you're going way out of you way to do this for me."

"No problem, Miss Heilman."

"Jenny, remember?"

"Okay, Jenny. Erik, remember?"

She smiled briefly and nodded her head. She had a pretty smile. Small white teeth.

"Erik with a K?"

"Yes, with a K, the German way."

"Are you German then?"

"No . . . no. Not for a long time."

"What do you mean?"

"Well, my Grandfather was born in Germany, but the Leidens sloughed off their ethnicity early on, I'm afraid. They wanted to be true-blue Americans. How about you? You have a German name too, Heilman."

"I didn't know it was German, and I don't know if I'm German or not."

"Really?"

"I never knew my parents. I'm . . . I'm kind of adopted, I guess. I've always had the name, though."

"Well, Jenny Heilman, we'll just consider you German in person as well as name, shall we? Welcome home." He motioned with his hand toward the snow blanketed countryside, nothing but snow, weighing down trees, turning small structures into white hummocks, most houses banked deeply on at least two sides, some up to the roof.

"Kind of a chilly reception," she said, pulling her thin windbreaker around her, but she was smiling. "I like it though. I've never seen snow, you know. This is really neat."

"Only because you're the passenger and don't have to drive in it."

She was silent for a long while, watching the whited countryside glide by, leaning against the door, her cheek against the glass.

He noticed the dark, low sky, and hoped that they would make it to Regensburg. The further north they drove, the more snow covered the highway, deeper tracks now where the car tires plowed through the powder. And then large flakes began to splat against the windshield.

"Is it snowing?" she asked, her whole face brightening.

"Afraid so." He turned on the wipers.

"Oh . . . oh," she cried. "Wonderful!" She clapped her hands softly as she watched the large fat flakes increase in number. "I've never seen it snow before."

"Don't get too excited. See all that snow plowed up beside the highway. Not so long ago, it was *on* the highway. That much snow falls again, and *we* won't be on the highway very long."

"Oh," was all she said, her hands caught in mid-clap.

The snow came in flurries, swirling and drifting, sometimes heavier, sometimes lighter, but always falling, falling. The wind keened and whipped the car, and he slowed to meet the conditions. Before long, though, the fall was steady and heavy, coming at them at a forty-five degree angle, the wipers on constantly, and the sky so dark that he checked the dash clock to make sure of the time.

The slush deepened on the roadway, and he tried to keep the tires in what was left of the narrow troughs left from previous traffic, but it became harder and harder to do, and he slowed even more. He had been surprised by the relative lack of traffic early on, but now he saw that the locals probably had more sense than he did. What should have taken no more than an hour or so in good weather would obviously take more than two, and by the time he saw the first signs for the A-92/A-3 Autobahn crossing, the snow fell and swirled with such force that he could hardly see, the wipers lugging with every slow sweep across the windshield, and from time to time the car seeming to take on a life of its own, drifting left or right at will. Regensburg was up the A-3 another seventy or so kilometers, and he wasn't sure that they would make it, and even if they did, he would surely never be able to get back here and then on up into the mountains to Bodenmais. The storm wasn't letting up -- it was getting worse.

"Listen, Jenny, we've got a problem here."

"Yeah, I kind of figured."

"I promised you I'd get you to Regensburg, but I'm not so sure we can even make it that far." He tried to pull off and stop alongside the highway so they could talk, but the snow was so deep that he jerked the wheel and pulled the car back into the more traveled path. "Shit!"

"So what do we do?"

"My turn-off is just across the A-3. You saw that sign back there. Deggendorf is where I pick up the road to Bodenmais. It's maybe forty kilometers from there to my hotel."

"How many miles? I didn't learn metrics, I'm afraid. Or much of anything else."

"Easy way is to multiply the kilometer by point six-two miles. So that's like twenty-four miles or so."

"Twenty-four point eight," she said a second later.

He raised an eyebrow. Maybe she didn't know metrics, but she obviously had a brain for math.

"So, what are you saying?" she said, scrunching up her forehead.

"Well, with any luck, maybe we'll make it to Bodenmais. At least our chances seem a lot better."

"Where does that leave me?" Her narrowed lavender eyes bored into him, and she turned toward him with her back against her door.

"Let me take you to my hotel. You can get a room for the night until the storm blows over, and then I promise you, I'll get you to Regensburg. I don't know what else to do, Jenny. This is a serious storm. I'm sure you can see the situation we're in."

"You know I don't have any money, Mr. Leiden. I can't just get a room for the night like you can." She turned and stared out the window. From the darkening sky snow fell so thickly that beyond the road only ghostly shapes and shadows moved slowly by.

"Don't worry about that, okay. I'll take care of the room. How about it?"

"I don't really have any choice, do I?" She didn't even look at him. "Seems like I never have any choice," she whispered into the window glass, fogging it with her words.

He put his hand out and touched her leg, but she jerked it away with her own. "I'm sorry," he said, unsure of whether he was apologizing for the touch or the circumstances, but he settled for the latter. "If I could think of anything else, I would."

A short while later she turned to him and touched his arm. "God, I must sound so ungrateful. I'm just so confused, Mr. Leiden . . . upset . . . whatever. I know none of this is your fault. You've been so nice to me and all, even though you think I'm some kind of Gothic weirdo." Her eyes shone with tears.

"I don't think of you --"

"That's okay. I know the way you looked at me on the plane, and still you helped me with my duffle. You're really a nice man. I'm sorry I've been so difficult for you."

That seemed such a long time ago already, and although it may have been true then, it certainly wasn't so any longer, was it?

"I don't think of you like that, Jenny. Not in the least," he said softly, trying to look sincere and hoping that he was.

She picked at her eyebrow ring and gave him a slight smile.

"I'm not going to force you to do anything. I just think this is the best we can do in a bad situation. Okay?"

She nodded, managed that half smile again, and shrugged those bird-like shoulders.

"Good, now we had better make some time while we still can. The regular highway may not be as clear of snow as the Autobahn. We don't want to get caught out in the middle of nowhere in this storm."

He took the Deggendorf exit, made his way through the town with her help, and managed to find Highway 11 toward Bodenmais. His fears were quickly confirmed as the car plowed through thick snow that hadn't been removed from the pavement. Even the Mercedes' four wheel positraction drive didn't make the task much easier, and he actually wondered just how far they would get. The snow on the pavement lacked the tire rutted tracks that the Autobahn had offered, and the car seemed to constantly pull this way and then that. It was clear that he had made the right choice, for he never would have gotten to Regensburg and back before this road would have been impassible. It was almost so as it was.

Less than twenty miles now, that's all they needed to cover, but here, off the Autobahn, night seemed to have closed in around them, the visibility cut to just a few feet in front of the car, a white curtain beyond. Huge drifts hemmed them in on either side of the road. Trees drooped beneath their white weight. Small buildings hunched, little more than blank mounds. The wipers strained to keep the cold accumulation of flakes pushed aside, and the engine whined every time the tires spun on unseen patches of ice. Already the muscles in his neck and shoulders roped and knotted, throbbed and ached, the tension running down his arms and into his hands as they gripped the wheel. The blue-green outdoor/indoor temperature gauge on the dash dipped from -13 grad to -14. He didn't really know how cold that was; he had never mastered the centigrade scale, but he guessed it was toward zero. Zero Celsius was 32 degrees Fahrenheit, wasn't it? He had been content to know that C. 30 was too hot, C. 25 was comfortable, C. 20 was a little cool, and anything below C. 10 was downright freezing. He knew that there was a clever way to figure the conversion by multiplying something by 9, but he could never remember what, and was normally content with his limited knowledge. This, however, was far from normal.

"You okay?" she asked him.

"Yes, why?"

"You're just so quiet."

"To tell the truth, driving in this sh -- stuff isn't easy. I keep telling myself, 'just a few more miles, just a few more miles.'" As he turned to look at her, the car veered toward the right shoulder, sideswiping the plowed up snow. "Shit!" He fought the wheel, let up on the gas, and fortunately the car found its way back into the center of the road.

"Sorry about that."

"Any idea how much farther it is?"

"Yes. Too far!"

3

He would have missed the sign if she hadn't called it to his attention. She thought they had already missed one a few kilometers back as it was. This one announced the town of Teisnach.

"Ah," he said, "I know this. We've already gone through Padersdorf, then. It really isn't much farther. Maybe two or three kilometers. We're going to make it, Jenny. I wasn't sure there for a while, but I think we're going to make it."

"Good," was all she said.

"But now you really have to help me. You have to be alert." The darkness had cut the visibility even more, and the light from the headlamps simply bounced off the snowfall that draped before them. More and more often the tires spun on patches of ice, and the car steered more like a boat than an auto. "There will be a sign on your side someplace before too long. It used to be green with three crowns on in, with the name *Die Drei Könige*, but the letters are in old script, so you probably won't be able to read them. Just look for a green sign with three crowns on it, okay?"

"Okay," she said, sitting forward on the seat, straining against the seatbelt, putting her hands on the dash. "It's really bad, isn't it?" she finally said. "I'm sorry I've been such a bother for you -- and you've been so nice about everything."

"Nonsense, Jenny. I would have been right here with or without you. I'm the one who should feel bad for dragging you away from where you want to go. And if this doesn't let up before long, you're not going to get there any time soon, I'm afraid."

"No problem. So I'm stranded a day or two. I'm still a lot closer than I was yesterday, right?"

"I suppose so, but I promise you that I will get you to Regensburg just as soon as humanly possible. You have my word on that."

"I know I do, Mr. Leiden. I know." She reached out and touched his arm, ran her fingers up and down the sleeve of his sport coat. "You've been so nice. I can't thank you enough."

Some time later, the snow still thicker, she cried, "There . . . there . . . the sign!"

"Good girl. I would have missed it for sure."

It was so dark and the snow fall so dense that the headlights did little more than defuse light throughout the swirling particles. Fortunately, she had seen the light green haze of the sign before they had passed it.

He had turned left a little too sharply, and the car drifted, but it was hard to tell just where the turn-off was, the snow plowed up almost evenly along the left shoulder. The bumper kicked up snow and the Mercedes dipped and then lunged, but he had little time to catch his breath. "Jesus," he said, having forgotten that the roadway down into the little valley of the *Drei Könige* was steep. "Hang on," he said, remembering the sharp bend in the road at the bottom of the grade, and then again, "Hang on!"

Even though her trianglular seat belt restrained her above and below the swell of her belly, he instinctively reached out and put his arm across her chest as he had done so many times when he had made a sudden stop with his young children riding in the front seat. "Shit! Shit! Shit!" He could feel the car drifting sideways, sliding down the steep incline, pushing up a mound of snow as it moved down the road on its own.

Beneath the powder the roadway must have been covered with ice, for even as the car moved sideways it picked up speed.

"God, Jenny! You okay?"

"Yeah, fine," she assured him.

"We're probably going to crash at the bottom of this hill. The road turns to the right, and I can't steer the damned car." And in that bright instant he thought of her unborn child. "Oh Christ," he muttered to himself, visions of decapitated infants, broken and lifeless children killed by the force of the very air-bags that were supposed to protect them flashed though his mind, and he quickly released his seatbelt and tried to hold her, to put himself between her and the dash, between the dash and her unborn baby, between the force of the exploding bag if it deployed and the life she carried.

In terrifying slow motion the tires eventually caught on the dirt shoulder, tilted the car sharply, and then it crashed into the snowbank with a muffled thud that shuddered the car and them with the near simultaneous ear-ringing deployment of the side air-bag, followed upon by the exploding front bags, Jenny screaming, digging her nails into his left arm, the force of the passenger side bag slamming against his back and side like a broad-headed sledge hammer, his body still managing somehow to slip between the two front bags, his right rib-cage kissed by the rim of the steering wheel with a sharp, flaring pain. And then they were caught in a moment of eerie silence, almost engulfed by the now silky billows of the fully deployed air-bags, the air dusted by fine, swirling white powder, and then they felt the wind buffeting the car.

"Christ, Jenny, are you okay?"

"I think so . . . yeah, I'm fine. Just shaken up." She squeezed the one arm that still clung to her.

"And the --"

"Yeah, we're both fine," she said and even managed a faint smile.

He could feel her entire body shaking. "I'm so sorry . . . I couldn't do anything . . . the car just . . . I don't know . . ."

"It wasn't your fault, Mr. Leiden. Anyway, it wasn't so bad, was it. I thought we were really going to get it. The snow sort of helped us, didn't it?"

"It seems like it. Just as long as you aren't hurt."

"I told you, I'm fine."

They both sat silently for a while, him aware only now that the engine was still running. He must have kicked the car out of gear in some way, he thought, and twisted around to turn off the ignition behind the driver's side air-bag. They could not so much hear the wind as feel it shake the car, slamming swirls of snow against the windows and metal body. As the air-bags began to deflate, he saw her hold out her hand and watch it tremble. He quickly took it in his own, but before he could say anything to her, she turned to him and said, "Another fine mess you've gotten us into." She squeezed his hand and smiled.

"Thanks a lot, but you're right." He stretched his smarting back and rubbed his neck. "No way are we getting this ox out of the ditch, Jenny. Afraid we're going to have to get to the hotel on foot."

"How far is it?"

"Oh, maybe a hundred yards or so farther."

"Oh boy."

"Let's leave the bags here for the night. We'll have a hard enough time getting ourselves there in this blizzard." He then tired to open his door, but it didn't budge.

"Can you open your door? Mine's either jammed or blocked."

"I'll try," she said, pulling the lever and nudging the door open with her elbow, but a fierce wind caught it and snapped it open with a whoosh and a snarl of freezing air and snow. "Jeeze . . . I can't . . . Oh!" She turned her back on the biting wind.

32

"Lean back," he said, making his way over the gearshift, over her, out from under the deflating air-bag and finally out the door. He managed to get the door shut, but it wasn't going to make it much warmer in the car now. He saw quickly that he had been right; the car was well wedged beneath the snow bank and far off the road. He shivered in his wool sportcoat, and knew that they would have to get to the hotel on foot and as quickly as they could. The car would not offer her warmth for long.

He opened the door a crack and fought to keep it just a crack, as the wind clawed at the opening. "Jenny! I'm sorry, but I was right. We'll have to walk. Can you reach back and get the coat out of my carry-on?"

She twisted and managed to unzip the bag, pulling out a heavy fleece lined parka. "Got it," she said.

"Well, put it on. You're going to freeze out here."

"What about you?"

"Forget about me. Just put the damned thing on. We have to hurry. It's freezing."

She didn't argue further, but slipped her arms into the sleeves, zipped it up and then he opened the door. The cold swallowed her in a wild swirl of snow. "Jeeze . . . jeeze . . . you've got to be --"

"Come on," he said, cutting her off. "We've got to move, Jenny. Not to scare you, but we've got to get to the hotel. We'll freeze out here in no time at all."

"I've really spoiled everything for you, haven't I."

"Shut up and walk, Jenny. We've got maybe a hundred yards of this shit to get through." He took her by the arm and began wading through the thick powdery snow that filled up the road between high ridges banked on either shoulder. "And you haven't spoiled a thing." The wind clawed through his wool jacket, and he tried to turn up the narrow collar. Well, maybe a few things, he thought.

After some time, bucking stiff headwinds, making little progress, he became aware that he couldn't feel his feet any longer. His expensive walking shoes didn't do a thing to keep out the cold. The girl leaned on him more and more, and then suddenly, as if felled by a freezing blow from the storm, she went down on one knee.

"I'm sorry, Mr. Leiden. I know you must be freezing, but I can't go any farther. I have to rest." She clung tightly to his arm, as if she were afraid that if she let go, he might disappear in a gust of blinding snow.

"Don't worry about me, Jenny, but I don't think we can rest. I don't have any sense of how far we still have to go, but I know it wouldn't take much to freeze to death out here."

"Leave me, then. Maybe you can send somebody back for me."

"That's bullshit, Jenny. I'm not leaving you. Stand up."

"But --"

"Stand up!"

She did, and he took her left arm and put it around his neck, then he bent and scooped her up in his arms.

"Oh! But you can't --"

"Oh, but I can," he said, and strode off, high-stepping, plowing through the snow with his double burden as best he could. Some time later, how much he had no sense, the snowfall seemed to lessen.

"Lights! I see lights, Mr. Leiden."

He could see them now as well, but they were probably not the lights of the hotel. He knew there were several houses along the road before one reached the *Drei Könige*, but he didn't say anything to her. Already he could feel muscles that had been numb before, burning with the strain. His breath blew ragged in uneven clouds and his lungs seemed to tear at their roots.

34

"You'll kill yourself," she said, hugging his neck. "I feel so bad. Put me down."

"I'm fine . . . just a little . . . ways to go," he wished more than knew, and then, just as he felt that he couldn't take another step, he saw through the snowy veil the shadowy bulk of the hotel with its muted, glowing windows. "There . . . Jenny . . . the hotel."

"Oh! Thank God -- thank *you*, Mr. Leiden."

After some time, he found the walk, obviously cleared earlier, but now thickly carpeted again, and the building blunted the wind, and its knifing ceased.

"I can walk now," she said, squeezing his neck in the crook of her arm. "You've done enough."

"Just to the . . . steps," he said, a new burst of energy flooding through his aching body.

"Oh, Erik, look at the windows!" As chilled and exhausted as she was, she noticed the decorated windows of the hotel, each lighted around the edges, decked with evergreens, all frosted for real by thick crystals of ice. "It's beautiful."

When he reached the foot of the steps that led to the double doors of the entryway, he put her down. "Careful . . . it may . . . be icy," he said through gasping breaths, aware of his age with regret. The steps themselves were lightly powdered with snow that had swirled up the steps.

Before she let go of his neck, she kissed him on the cheek. "You've been wonderful, Mr. Leiden. I would have been lost without you."

"Well . . . you almost were . . . with me," he said, breath still coming in ragged gasps, and he held her arm as they made their way up the steps. He pulled open one of the heavy outer doors which was so tightly sealed that it opened with an audible whoosh as the couple stepped into the entryway.

"Double doors?" she said.

"They have lots of . . . cold weather. Helps keep . . . the inside warm," and then he pulled open the inner door. They were met by a wall of warm, fragrant air.

"Oh, heaven!" she cried. Warmth!"

"*Mein Gott!*" cried a stout, rosy-cheeked woman standing just inside the door, her blond hair streaked with gray. She wore a loose white blouse, the neck slightly ruffled, the short sleeves puffed, and a full patterned skirt of dark green, much of it covered by a apron of paler green that hung from her thick waist.

"Frau Holzman," he said to her. "*Ich freue mich, Sie wiederzusehen.*" Under the circumstances he was more than glad to see her again. He shook snow from his hair, from his clothing, and stamped his feet on the rough carpet inside the door.

"*Ich auch,* Herr Leiden. It has been far too long ago."

"Yes, I agree." He still gasped for breath.

Then she seemed to notice the girl for the first time, and looked from one to the other. Catching herself, she looked at him and said in English, "We are . . . how do you say . . . 'giving up' on you. The weather is horrible, *nicht wahr?*" She lapsed back into German. "But how did you get here?" she asked, as though the impossibility of the situation had just dawned on her.

"*Mit dem Auto, aber das ist im Schnee . . .* ah . . ." He didn't know the word. "How do you say "stuck" in German? *Festgeklebt?*"

"Yes, yes, I understand. Your car is stuck in the snow. But how did you get here? By foot?"

"Only from the turn in the road," he said. He was tired, and his German, as rusty as it was, wouldn't come as he wanted. He said nothing of carrying her for much of the way.

"*Ach!* How awful! Poor man. But now you are here. Come," she said, more to the girl than him. "You are almost frozen, yes? Stand at the fire." She led her to the fireplace. While Frau Holzman talked with him, the girl drifted closer to the glorious heat that leapt and crackled in the hotel's large, fieldstone fireplace. There were chairs and couches around the fire, some occupied, others not, but she stood by the low hearth and warmed first her hands, then turned and warmed her back. The guests stared at her, but in his large coat no one would have known that she was pregnant.

"Are you together?" asked Frau Holzman, as they stood to one side.

He smiled at her. "No. No. Nothing like that. Actually, I was giving her a ride to Regensburg when the storm got so bad that I decided I had better come straight here. She needs a room of her own."

"*Ach!* Herr Leiden. *Tut mir leid*, I am sorry, but we have no rooms free. The season and all the snow, you know. We are filled to the . . . what . . . beams?"

"Nothing is free then? How about another hotel near? Or perhaps a local *Zimmerfrei?*"

"I think not, Herr Leiden. Everything is now difficult. I am so sorry." She began walking toward the reception desk of dark, polished wood behind which the room keys hung above their pigeon-hole boxes.

"Is there a couch in my room?" he asked as he followed her.

"Yes, a small one. What do you call it, a lover's seat?"

"Yes, a loveseat. Wait a minute, Frau Holzman. I'd better check with her." He motioned for her to come to the desk.

"It's lovely, Mr. Leiden. The Christmas tree is the most beautiful I've ever seen." She looked at the large fir standing in one corner, strung not only with countless colored lights, each with its own small foil reflector, but also adorned with ornaments of every size and description, glass globes, hand-carved animals of every kind, elaborate nut-crackers, and angels, so many angels, of all shapes and sizes.

"We've got a little problem, Jenny. Mrs. Holzman says that they are full up. No more rooms. Mine is the last."

"Oh," was all she said, her smile slowly fading.

"Relax, they're not going to put you out in the storm, but you'll have to share my room. There is a couch of sorts, she says, but I'm afraid it's a loveseat."

"As long as it's warm, Mr. Leiden. I don't think I'll complain," she said. "If you don't mind me being there, I don't mind."

"Okay, then." He turned back to Frau Holzman and said, "I'm afraid all the luggage is still in the car."

"No problem. Johann can take the snowmobile with the sled."

"Thank you." He handed her the keys to the Mercedes. "It's the gray one stuck in the snow," he said by way of a joke and they both laughed.

"We will go up to the room, and then in a little while, is it still possible to get some dinner?" He really had no idea of the hour.

"The kitchen is closed, Herr Leiden, but for you we will manage something. Just let us know when you are coming down."

"Good."

And then they walked along a gayly lit and decorated hallway toward the stairs. Small fir trees trimmed with their own small lights and wreathed and spangled with foil ribbons and blown glass ornaments stood at intervals along the way, and golden angles gauzed in gossamer hung from the ceiling.

"It's really beautiful. Just like Christmas should be. And that smell. What is it? It's wonderful."

"Well," he said, lifting his nose with exaggerated sniffing. "Some gingerbread -- *Lebkuchen,* some spiced cider, hard, I'm afraid, some *Glühwein* -- mulled or spiced wine, the Germans love that at Christmas time, but it's far too sweet for me, and let's see, *Schweinebraten*, roast pork, if you want to know the truth, and then behind it all, the redolent smell of fresh fir."

"Gee."

"Come on. Let's wash up. I'm starving."

"Oh, good. Me too. Both of us!"

At the top of the stairs he switched on a light which brightened the dark hall. "The Germans are very conservation conscious. They don't waste resources. That light will stay on for about two or three minutes, and then turn off automatically."

"Boy, are they wasting a lot of electricity downstairs then."

"Ah, Jenny, it's Christmas. They make a grand exception. They go all out at *Weihnachtszeit* here. That's one of the reasons I've always wanted to be here at this time." Not alone, though, he reminded himself.

"Where are we going? The rooms don't have any numbers?"

"No, every room has its own name. We are headed for *das Schwalbennest*, down at the end of the hall, a large corner room with a fantastic view -- when the weather is good, that is."

"And what does the name mean?"

"The swallow's nest."

"I like that. The swallow's nest. Do you feel like a swallow? I kind of do."

"I feel more like a bear, Jenny. I am famished."

At the end of the hall, he stopped before a dark wooden door that had an oval brass plate spelling out the name of the room in fancy script. "By the way, these are European locks. If you've never had a room with one, you can lock yourself out. Just remember, you have to turn the key all the way around twice. Twice around, okay?"

She nodded and followed him through the door. He flipped a switch and a soft light bathed the entryway. "Another German trait. To conserve electricity, the wattage of their bulbs is much lower than ours. No problem here, though. The *Drei Könige* has lots of lamps and even overhead lights." He flipped another switch and the overhead fixture in the middle of the ceiling and two wall mounted lamps illuminated the entire room.

"My gosh! It's so big, and so . . . nice." She walked around, looking at and touching everything.

The entryway opened onto a landing of sorts, a sitting room where a table and two chairs sat. Two cloths covered the table, a pale green beneath a white laid at right angles, so that the edge made alternating white and green triangles. Beyond the table, against the wall stood a desk and another chair. The loveseat, a pale green velvet, stood against the opposite wall. She stepped down into the bedroom and looked at the large bed, its headboard a washed blond that revealed the wood grain beneath. Hand painted red and white flowers covered the wood, bordered by curling green vines. She walked over to the large armoire across from the bed and ran her hand up and down the smooth warm wood. It displayed the same blooms and leafy vines. She moved back to the bed, really two separate, smaller beds side by side. Each had its own mattress secured in a wooden frame, and each had its own thick, cream-colored comforter, quilted in large connecting ovals, with the top third turned back to form a divided pyramid. The sheets beneath were pale green. She ran her fingers lightly along the comforter. At the head of each leaned two huge, fluffy pillows, and atop the first lay a small foil wrapped bar.

"Chocolate?" she asked.

"Yes, and it's very good."

"I've never been in such a wonderful place. If I pinch myself, I'll probably wake up." She walked around and around. "And it's warm, too," she said, smiling broadly, hugging herself.

He was aware that when she smiled, she was really rather pretty, even with the powdered pallor, rings and purple tinted hair. He realized that he hadn't really given her much of a chance in the beginning. "Why don't you go on and use the bathroom first."

"If you don't mind. I have to pee really bad."

It suddenly dawned on him that she hadn't used a restroom in hours. She had needed to use rest stops along the Autobahn twice, which had annoyed him then, but there hadn't been any such thing once they had begun their trek along Highway 11. He sat down on the bed and waited. He could almost feel the tension draining from his neck and shoulders, the warmth coming back into his body, especially into his tingling feet. He had never gone though anything quite like that before, and he didn't care to ever again.

"Wow, this is really something. I've never been in such a nice bathroom," she said from behind the closed door.

And then he could hear her peeing into the toilet. It had been a long time since he had heard that sound. Funny to be hearing it now, here, in such circumstances. Life was strange. Then he heard the tap running.

"Jeeze, the water's like ice."

"There's hot water too."

"Oh! It just kicked in." In a moment she came out smiling again. "This just doesn't seem real, you know?"

"My turn," he said. He had forgotten how nice the bathroom really was. The pale green tile, the towel warmers, the oversized tub, the double basins set in a counter top of pale green marble. For an inexpensive family run hotel, the *Drei Könige* was just about as good as it got.

4

Later, they sat in the cozy *Bierstube* waiting for the eldest son Torsten to prepare a *Bauernfrühstück*. The room was somewhat crowded, people having left the dining room and made their way down for a night of drinking and socializing, words almost synonymous for many Germans, he had explained to her. The room's knotty pine gave it warmth, and antique farm, timber and mining implements hanging from the walls gave it charm. Most of the people seemed older, Jenny being the youngest by far.

"So come on, what's this Bowerstuk we're having?" She sipped the hot spiced apple juice he had ordered for her.

He spelled the word out for her. "Farmer's breakfast. Diced fried potatoes, ham, onions, scrambled eggs, salt and pepper." He sipped from a tall glass of dark beer.

"Fried?"

"Afraid so."

"I try not to eat fried foods, you know. For the baby."

"Well, you try it, and if it's not to your liking, maybe we can get you something else. Herr Holzman's is the best I've ever had, though, and I've had lots. It's a dish that is often very greasy; here it isn't. Just try it, okay?"

"Okay, but I don't know."

He took a drink from his tall, dark beer.

"You like beer?" she asked him, wrinkling up her nose.

"Yes, I love beer, and this is one of the best in the world." He caught himself, smiled and said, "At least, it's one of my favorites. *Klosterbrauerei Scheyern Dopplebock Dunkel.*" He took another long swallow. It was just as good as he remembered it. And it had to be a long ago memory, for the small brewery on the outskirts of Erding didn't export.

"Boy is that a mouthful. To me beer tastes like . . . horse piss."

"Sampled a lot of horse piss, have you?"

She shrugged and smiled. "I heard someone say that once. I liked it. I just know beer tastes awful."

"Well, maybe you just haven't tasted the right beer."

"Maybe." She drank her hot apple juice. "Is this the spiced cider you said you smelled?"

"No, the cider is hard. I knew you didn't drink. That's just apple juice heated and spiced up a bit."

"Thanks. All you seem to do is take care of me. I can't thank you enough, Mr. Leiden."

"Well, one thing you can do is stop calling me Mr. Leiden. We're sharing a room together, for God's sake. You could at least call me Erik."

"I'll try, but it feels funny."

Just then an older woman in white blouse and black skirt came to their table carrying a huge oval platter heaped with their dinner. "So," she said, placing a large fork and spoon into either end of the mounded, steaming mass. With a wide, snaggle-toothed smile, she said, *"Noch etwas,* Herr Leiden?"

"Thank you, no, Greta. Nothing else."

"Guten Appetit!" she said, turning to leave, and stopping. "Herr Leiden, *gut dass Sie wieder da sind."*

"Thanks. I am glad, too."

"What did she say?" Jenny asked.

"She just said that it was good that I was back."

She gave him a quizzical look. "Are you somebody famous or something?"

He laughed out loud, so loud that others turned to look at them.

"No . . . no, not at all."

43

"But everybody is so nice to you."

"I used to come here a lot in the old days, but it has been a number of years since I've been here."

"Well, they sure must like you," she said and then paid attention to the food. "There is so much," she said, eyes wide. "And it smells so good."

"I promise you it will taste even better. Can I serve you, or do you want to serve yourself?"

"If you want to, but not too much. If it's too greasy, I don't want to eat a lot."

He took her blue and white dinner plate, the state colors of Bavaria, he had told her, and spooned a small portion of the steaming dish onto it.

"A caution! I know you're concerned about your diet. The Germans tend to use lots of salt, especially out in country inns and hotels like this, so you'd better taste your food before you add anything. Anyway, you'll have to ask, because the salt and pepper isn't usually on the table."

She already had a forkful on the way to her mouth. "Mmmmmm," she mumbled as she chewed.

He heaped his own plate, and ate eagerly. When had they eaten last? Well before landing in Frankfurt, a light breakfast of sorts, a roll and cold cuts, some yogurt. That had to be almost twelve hours ago. No wonder they were starving. He watched her eat, and took satisfaction in it.

"I don't believe this is just kind of fried potatoes and scrambled eggs, right? It's yummy. Can I help myself?"

"Glad you like it. Not too greasy for you?"

"Well, if it is, it's just once, right? I can't resist."

"I know. It's one of my favorite things to eat here. 'Peasant food,' my ex-wife used to say."

"Oh, I thought you were . . . you know . . . married."

"Not any more. Not for a long time now." What was it, five, no six years in January. It seemed like forever, and then again, only yesterday.

"I'm sorry. It's none of my business. I don't know what's gotten in to me. I don't usually talk very much."

"Don't worry about it. Old wounds. Lots of scar tissue."

She pushed the last morsels onto her fork with a finger, put them into her mouth and chewed quietly, and then looked at him in a strange way. "When I was little, they thought I was maybe autistic or something. I just never talked. I talk more now, though, since the baby is coming. I have to, you know. I don't want her to be like me."

"What do you mean, 'like you'. And just what's the matter with you."

"I'm a fuck-up. I know that. And I'm pretty stupid, too -- no, not really stupid, more like ignorant, I guess. Yeah, I'm really ignorant. You'd be amazed at what I don't know. I didn't study in school -- never graduated. Dropped out in the 10th grade. I don't want that for my baby. I want him or her to have a chance, a better chance than I had. I have to be able to talk about things with them." Then she was silent.

He knew that there was much more to Jenny Heilman than he had ever suspected, but she obviously wasn't going to expose any more of herself then, and he sure wasn't going to pry. The waitress returned.

"*Noch etwas*, Herr Leiden?"

"No, I don't think so, Greta." And then he asked the girl, "Would you like something else, Jenny, or are you finished?"

"My God, I don't think I've ever eaten so much, but it was so good. I just couldn't stop." She took the cloth napkin and wiped the corners of her mouth. The black lipstick had almost disappeared, giving her face a softer look.

"We are both fine, thank you. It was delicious -- as usual," he said in German, and she began clearing away their dishes.

45

"Dessert?" Greta asked in strained English.

"How about it?" he asked the girl. "They make wonderful *Strudel*, and a Bavarian cream that's -- what do you ladies say, 'to die for'."

"Oh, I wish I could," she said with a frown, "but I am absolutely stuffed. Baby doesn't leave me much room, you know."

"*Nein, danke.*"

"Anything else to drink, Herr Leiden?"

"Yes, a *Kirschbrand* maybe. Jenny, do you want some more hot apple juice or maybe a mineral water? I'm having a brandy."

"I just don't have room, Mr. . . . ah, Erik."

"*Nur den Brand,*" he said to the waitress.

"*Gut.*" She left carrying the platter, plates, and silverware.

"The Holzmans have their own distillery. They make *Kirschwasser*, *Mirabellenwasser*, *Schnaps* and brandies of all kinds, and the cherry one that I ordered is their house specialty."

"You know a lot about that stuff, don't you?"

"That stuff?"

"Yeah, like wine and beer, that kind of thing."

"Yes, I guess I do."

"How come?"

"I'm an importer. I also used to have several wine and spirits shops in southern California. Now I just have a small one in Brentwood, on San Vicente, The Wine Merchant, do you know it?"

"No, I don't know anything about wine, or much of anything else. Even before the baby, I wasn't much of a drinker." She was quiet for a while, and then picked up the thread she had dropped. "So you just travel all over buying wine and stuff."

"Well, I used to travel all over, but I haven't done that in a long time. I suppose I got too big. I could afford to pay other people to do it for me."

"But you said you only have a small shop now."

"Long story, Jenny, long, long story, and you don't want to hear the gruesome details, I assure you. Anyway, it's late, and if you are as tired as I am, we need to head on up to the room. I also need a shower in the worst way."

"Oh, me, too," she said. "I must smell just awful."

Her directness both unnerved and charmed him. Such directness was a rarity in the circles in which he moved. Maybe he should take a lesson or two from young Jenny Heilman, if it was not too late.

As they got up from the table, a young man dressed in black and white checked pants and a white cook's tunic, one side of the collar thrown open rakishly, came out of the kitchen. "Herr Leiden," he called.

"Torsten!"

"So good of you to see," the young man said, brushing his thick brown hair off of his forehead and offering his hand.

"Me too, Torsten."

"Jenny, this is Torsten, Frau Holzman's oldest son."

"Hello," she said, suddenly shy.

"Hallo," he said. "Sorry, mein English ist not so gut. *Können wir deutsch sprechen,*" he said to him.

"But of course you can speak German."

He told Torsten that the food had been excellent, which was no surprise to him, and Jenny moved away as they continued talking for a bit. Torsten told him that he did most of the cooking now, his father the overseer of the kitchen. Even Johann, the younger brother, cooked a lot.

"You are tired, yes?" Torsten finally said.

"Yes, I am tired, a long day," he said, taking Jenny's arm. "*Bis morgen.*"

"Yes, till tomorrow," the young man said in English as they left the dining area.

In the room they discovered that someone, Johann probably, had delivered their luggage. Her blue duffle sat beside his huge suitcase and carry-on bag.

"Why don't you go ahead and shower, or do whatever you're going to do, Jenny. I'll wait."

"You don't mind?"

"No, you go ahead. Would you like me to go out until you've finished?"

"I've already inconvenienced you enough, Mr. Leiden. I don't mind you staying if you don't --. I really don't think you'd --" but she just shook her head. "Nothing. It was stupid."

"Okay, I'll just stretch out for a bit." He sat down on the far side of the bed and slipped off his shoes, then lay back with his hands laced behind his head. She was still standing there looking at him with a slight frown. "Go on," he nudged, which she did.

Had she expected to get the bed? There was no way he could fit on the couch, even she probably wouldn't. She closed the door and in a few minutes he heard the shower running. A bit late for a shower in a German hotel, but they would just have to endure it for one night.

As he lay there, fragments of the day floated by. At the time it had seemed a rather horrid affair, but now, it was just . . . well, it just was. He was here, and it felt good, even under the circumstances. What circumstances? Hell, it was even kind of nice having her around. What would he have been feeling had he been alone? His thoughts tumbled out of their container and spilled across the Atlantic, washed across the continent, and lapped up into the dry Los Angeles basin, but the next thing he knew, he heard his name being called, some sweet voice out of the dark calling him.

"Mr. Leiden . . . Mr. Leiden, are you awake? Erik!"

"Hoooaah," he said with a start, his body jerking up. "Sorry, drifted off."

"I'm all done. The shower was yummy, but now I'm really sleepy."

He turned and looked at her. "Wow," he said softly to himself.

"Wow what?"

No nose ring. No eyebrow ring. No studs down and around her ear. No white mask -- face scrubbed now down to a smooth olive complexion. And the black bob -- not a trace of purple, the damp hair hugging her skull like a cap. She stood there wrapped in one of the *Drei Könige's* large fluffy bath towels, her shoulders thin and bare, the hollows behind her raised collarbones deep, her neck long and graceful.

"God, Jenny, you are . . . you are . . ." He couldn't say the word that leapt to his tongue; it was too troubling. "You look so different."

"I didn't want to embarrass you any more. I know how the people looked at us downstairs, and I know this place is somehow really special for you. It sure would be for me. I just want you to know how much I appreciate everything you have done for me. You are the nicest man I've ever met. I know what you did in the car, too. It was for my baby. And then you carried me all that way. You were wonderful."

He was shaking his head at her, one eyebrow raised. "You'd better check that out with my ex-wife, Jenny. I imagine she'd beg to differ with you."

"It's true. Even the baby's father. Now I think maybe he wasn't so nice after all. Nothing like you, at least. I wish I could repay you for all your kindness, but I know I can't."

"Nonsense, Jenny. You're a good girl. I've enjoyed your company."

"Now I really have to go to sleep. I can hardly keep my eyes open."

"I would offer you the bed, Jenny, but there is no way I can sleep on that loveseat. You probably won't accept my suggestion, but if you wanted, you could have half the bed -- it's really two, you know. Your own comforter and everything. And if you are concerned, about me, you really needn't be. I can promise you you'd be safe. I'm just about the most old-fashioned man you'll ever meet. A real throw-back. Don't believe in casual sex. Was absolutely faithful to my wife for the nearly twenty-five years we were together. Absolutely monogamous. One of us had to be, I suppose. And certainly not a child molester. But you do what you're comfortable doing."

"I trust you, Mr. Lei -- Erik. I really do. And I'm not a child," she said sternly. "Anyways, I know I'm not very tempting in my condition." She ran the palm of her right hand around her terry clothed belly.

"Don't kid yourself, Jenny Heilman. You would tempt any man, whatever your condition."

She smiled at him, even blushed. "You're just so nice. But I'd really feel funny in bed with you -- not *you*, you, just any you. Understand?"

"Sure do. Sleep tight, Jenny. I'll see you in the morning."

"*Bis morgen.* Is that right?"

"My, my, are you the quick one. Yes, until tomorrow. You'll be fluent in a day or two at this rate."

He brushed his teeth, shaved, and showered. It did feel good, the hot water beating on his neck and shoulders, washing away the last of the day's tensions. Even though he was tired, he felt oddly contented, strangely snug here in the *Drei Könige* again, a place he had always felt at home. When he came out

50

of the bathroom, she was curled up on the loveseat, the cream comforter wrapped around her, the only thing showing, the dark sheen of her short hair. For such a shitty day, it had all ended rather well he thought as he climbed into bed and turned out the light. Her soft breathing came to him from the sitting room, deep and even, a sound somehow comforting, so comforting that even as shadowy thoughts attempted to climb the edges of his consciousness, they failed to find purchase and slipped back into the inky darkness. Then without warning a different kind of darkness washed over him, enveloped him in his own soft, deep sleep.

5

He awoke slowly, a bubble rising through the viscous dark.
The awareness of heat came before the sense of flesh. Then
the struggle to make sense of it, the smooth bottom and back
he spooned against. The room swam in half-light, and then the
bits and pieces began to attract one another, began to coalesce.
Miss Heilman . . . Jenny! It all finally quivered, shimmered
and came together with an electric snap. Sometime during the
night she had obviously left the loveseat, had probably grown
uncomfortable, and now slept beside him. Her tee shirt had
ridden up around her hips, the front of his thighs now snug
against the back of her own, the round heat of her buttocks
firm against his . . . his . . . Christ, he was hard, too hard. He
eased back from her warmth as quickly but as quietly as he
could. As he rolled onto his back and away from her, she
uttered a soft sigh but then snuggled beneath her comforter as
if seeking a lost heat of her own. At least he had had enough
sense to wear his pajamas, something he didn't always do. He
turned on his left side to look at his travel alarm and saw the
green digital numbers glowing 9:33 am.

He couldn't remember when he had last slept to such an
hour, and as the thought sank in, so did the need for his
morning coffee, some three hours late by clock time, but who
knew how many by body time. Fortunately the separated
mattresses of the German double bed left her undisturbed as he
got up quietly, went into the bathroom, dressed quickly and
went downstairs.

When he returned shortly, carrying a tray with a small pot of coffee and one of hot chocolate and two glasses of juice, he found her sitting up in bed crying. "Are you all right?" he asked, setting the tray down on the desk.

"Yes. Now."

"What's the matter?" he asked, walking over to the bed.

"Nothing," she said, sniffling.

"God, don't say 'nothing'. My wife used to drive me crazy saying that."

"I woke up . . . and you . . . you were gone," she said between sobs.

"I just went down for coffee, and some hot chocolate for you."

"I see . . . but I thought . . . you were *gone* gone. I thought you had left me." In the semi-darkness he could see that she held her hands in front of her face.

"Jenny, Jenny. You still don't trust me, do you? I told you I would get you where you want to go, didn't I. I promised you. I may not be much, but I like to think I'm a man of my word."

"I'm sorry. I guess I just get silly sometimes. That's really not like me at all, but since I've been pregnant, I get upset all the time. Cry all the time. I'm usually very controlled."

"That's normal, Jenny. I remember my ex-wife's pregnancies."

"I know, but I still don't like it. Now I'm just a mess."

"You're anything but a mess, Jenny. It's all okay now, though, right? I'm going to stay right here. I assumed you didn't want coffee, so I brought you some hot chocolate and some juice."

"Thank you." She wiped her tears with the backs of her hands and tried to smile.

"They had apple and grape. Didn't know which you'd like, so I brought a glass of both. Germans drink a lot of fruit juice, and it's usually very good."

"You are such a sweet man, Mr. Leiden. I don't know what I would have done without you."

"Probably gotten yourself to Regensburg somehow instead of being stuck with me here."

"For sure!"

"Hot chocolate?"

"Well, okay." She took the bottom corner of her mouth between her teeth while he poured the rich chocolate from the small silver pot into a blue and white china cup, and then carried it to her.

"Almost breakfast in bed," he said as he handed it to her.

"As close as I've ever come," she said. "Is is still snowing?"

"Yes, but at least the wind isn't blowing like it was. Shall I open the drapes?"

She nodded, sipped her chocolate, and uttered a muted, "Oh! It's hot, but good," she added. "Thank you."

"You're welcome," he said as he opened the heavy, dark green drapes, a weak light spilling into the room. "It's pretty out."

"Let me see," she said, getting up carefully so as not to spill her chocolate.

She wore a long, oversized blue tee shirt that fell to mid-thigh. Her high, round belly tented it before her, and he couldn't help but notice her thin but shapely legs. Yes, what man wouldn't be tempted by her. He had a troubling flashback to his first waking sensations.

She moved to the window and stood beside him. "It's like a Christmas card," she said, looking at the snow covered hills, the thick firs weighed down, all gauzed in a steady fall of white.

"Yes, but I don't think we'll be going any place today. Frau Holzman said it is supposed to snow throughout the day, getting worse toward evening. Sorry."

"It's okay. Really." She put her hand on his shoulder. "We're starving, by the way."

"Good, me too. You two get ready, and we'll go down for some breakfast."

"*Frühstück*," she said, grinning.

"You are a clever girl, aren't you?"

She shrugged her shoulders and headed for the bathroom, after taking another brief sip of her hot chocolate and a long drink of apple juice.

Downstairs smelled different, but just as heavenly as it had the night before. This time they didn't go down into the *Bierstube*, but into the main dining room where a large buffet was set up along the far end. The room was large, the ceiling high with dark wooden beams running lengthwise. The tall windows would have flooded the room with sunlight at any other time. This morning they needed help from the lamps that burned along the walls and from the elaborate iron fixtures that hung from the sturdy beams.

"Oh my God! I've never seen so much food."

There were yogurts of several kinds in large crystal bowls, several varieties of fruit, cereal grains to mix, rolls and breads of all kinds in huge wicker baskets, jams, jellies, great corrugated curls of yellow butter floating in water, sausages, and sausages, and still more sausages, thinly sliced hams, and cold cuts without end. In a small basket covered with a thick blue and white checked cloth she found boiled eggs.

"Normally breakfast would be over by now, but the weather has kept every one in, apparently. The breakfast hours have been extended. Lucky us."

"Oh yes, lucky us. We just help ourselves?"

"Yes, but let's find our table first. It will have our name on it." They finally found it next to a large green and white tiled stove that came right out of the wall. The card said, "*Herr Leiden u. Gast*".

"Mr. Leiden and what?" she asked.

"Guest."

"Oh."

"They've put us by the *Kachelofen*. That's the tiled stove. It's very old. It came from a palace in Passau."

"It's warm, that's for sure. Nice."

They went back to the buffet. Small plates, large plates, ceramic and glass bowls of various sizes were stacked at the left end of the buffet table. Oblong wicker baskets lined with linens held the silverware.

"I don't know what to do," she said, looking at him with a shrug of her shoulders.

"What would you like?"

"Maybe some yogurt."

"What kind?"

"I don't know. What do they have?"

"I imagine this is cherry, this berry, maybe raspberry, this one peach, and that plain."

"I'll try the cherry."

"Take one of the small glass bowls and help yourself." Each large crystal bowl had a silver serving spoon in it.

From the baskets of rolls and breads, everything from thick, unsprouted rye and wheat to light and airy bleached semolina flour rolls, he helped her find a whole-grained bread, then several slices of nice lean ham, a soft boiled egg, and finally a bowl of the ubiquitous *Müsli*. After he had taken her back to the table, he loaded up his own plate with fried sausages, fried eggs, rolls and a variety of cold cuts.

"How do you stay so trim?" she asked when he sat down his plate.

"I don't eat like this all the time, that's for sure. But I love it, so when I am here, I indulge myself."

A young girl in a black, rustling skirt and white puffy blouse came and asked, *"Kaffee, Tee, oder Schokolade?"*

"What will it be for you?" he asked her. "More hot chocolate?"

"It was really good," she said, "but maybe some herbal tea if they have it."

"Wasn't the hot chocolate okay?"

"It was fine, Mr. Leiden, but chocolate has . . . has caffeine in it. I try not to drink anything with caffeine in it."

"I'm sorry, Jenny. I didn't know that about the chocolate."

"Why should you? You're not pregnant. Don't feel bad about it, okay. You are the most thoughtful man I've ever known."

"How about some camomile tea, then? I know they have that. Up north, toward the Baltic, there are acres and acres of rolling farmland planted in camomile. On hot summer days the air is redolent with the smell. The farmers there must be a very relaxed lot, huh?"

She smiled and said, "Camomile will be fine."

He ordered the tea for her and a small pot of coffee for himself.

"Everything is so good, and the bread is heavenly. I could just live on this. It's like eating manon or something," she said, as she tore a piece off the thick slice of dark bread and dipped it into her yogurt, and he didn't correct her.

She rolled up a slice of ham with her fingers and took a bite. "I'll bet this is bad for me -- us, but it tastes really good."

"The food in Germany is usually quite good, simple, but quite good. The Holzman's though, now theirs is a cut above."

"I see why you like it here."

That and the fact that his wife had never been there with him, he mused. The Bavarian Forest and the *Drei Könige* were too backwoods for her, too *altdeutsch*. She had been a woman to the city born. Munich. Düsseldorf. Hamburg. She had put up with them. That was if she were forced to be in the country in the first place. She found the language horrible, the food barely tolerable, and the people backward. Most often she had preferred to stay in France or Switzerland while he did his work in Germany.

He enjoyed watching Jenny eat. Every morsel was a delight to her, and she didn't hide her satisfaction. She went back for more yogurt and bread, but returned with several more slices of pale pink ham besides.

He raised an eyebrow.

"It's really lean and almost paper thin. It won't be that bad, will it?"

He just smiled at her, sipping at another cup of strong German coffee. There were only a few people left in the dining room, and he was in no hurry to leave. What would they do, go back to the room? Then what? He hoped that this didn't become difficult just because of their proximity.

"You really like Christmas, huh?" drawing him back.

"Ah . . . yes, yes, I love Christmas. And you don't?"

"Not a whole bunch." She was cleaning her yogurt bowl with her last piece of bread. "Why do you like it so much?"

"Oh, I don't know. I've always loved it, even as a little kid. I have all these wonderful memories, vivid as hell, when I was little. The bright lights. The smell of the tree. The presents all wrapped and shiny with ribbons and bows. And the goodies, I suppose. Candy. Chocolates. Divinity. Fudge. My German grandmother's *Pfeffernüsse* -- hard little anise cookies I ate by the handsful, and *Stollen*, a little like a fruit cake, but lighter and delicious. And there were parties, and lots of relatives and friends. Everything was special, then. Nothing was ordinary. Christmas shopping was charged in some wonderful way, and I always tried to find the right gift for my folks. I saved my allowance for the last half of the year, usually."

"You would, wouldn't you?" she said almost to her self.

"It seemed like everybody was happier at that time of year. People on the streets, in the stores, everywhere. Now it all seems pretty hectic. Nobody having much fun. Hell, maybe I just have selective memory. What's your most memorable Christmas?" he asked her.

"No, you're the one who likes Christmas, you tell me."

"Ummmm, that's hard. I guess I'd have to pick either the Christmas I was seven or the one when I was thirteen. When I was seven I got this wonderful electric train -- from Germany! I had forgotten that. It was great, though. All the bells and whistles, chugging along and puffing smoke, the whole thing. Funny thing was, I heard it before I even saw it, that electric humming, the clickity-clack of the wheels on the track. My young heart raced in time with its little motor, and then I saw it churning around this huge figure eight set-up. I gave it to my boys when they were about that age, but they were never much interested in it." He was silent for a long time, finished his coffee and pushed back from the table a bit. "Now you."

"No, you have one more, when you were thirteen."

"You really can't be interested in this, can you?"

"Oh, but I am. I like hearing you talk, and it all sounds so wonderful." She had pushed back her plate and sat with her elbows on the table, and her chin resting on top of her laced fingers. "Go on."

"I got a rifle, .22. I didn't think I would, even though my folks knew I wanted one. They didn't approve of guns, but I guess my begging for it had worn them down. I had a BB gun, but I wanted a real gun. And there it was beneath the tree Christmas morning, the wooden stock gleaming beneath the colored lights, the dark barrel shining. I knew how hard it must have been for them to do that. I guess that's why it sticks in my mind."

"What happened to it?"

"I still have it, packed away. I only used it once, if you want to know the truth. We lived out in the country then, and I went squirrel hunting with my dog. Even though I had no real practice firing it, I guess it was enough like the BB gun that the first shot I took, I killed a squirrel. When I found it, all bloody and still quivering, I knew that I could never do that again. That was the last time I ever fired it. My folks never said a word." Another sip of coffee, and then, "Okay, now your turn. Your most memorable Christmas."

Without the hint of a smile, she pushed her chair back and said, "I really don't have one, Mr. Leiden. Christmas has always been a real downer for me, if *you* want to know the truth," she said, echoing his words. She got up and left the table with him sitting there, coffee cup still in hand.

6

He found her some time later sitting on the hearth before the fireplace, her arms wrapped around her stomach, one above, the other below, as though she were holding her unborn baby, or maybe protecting it. He had no idea whether she wanted to be left alone or not, and his first instinct was to go back to the room, but on second thought he joined her beside the fire. She had obviously been crying, but she wasn't any longer.

"I'm sorry if I upset you, Jenny. I sure didn't intend to, but if I did, I apologize."

"It's not your fault, Mr. Leiden. I told you I'm a mess right now. It's like all my nerves are raw or something. You rub me the wrong way, and I just react. Don't worry, you didn't do anything. You're the sweetest, gentlest man I've ever met. I think I know you would never hurt me. You just made me think about stuff I try real hard never to think about."

"Well, I'm sorry for making you think about it, then." He put his arm around her shoulders and gave her a hug.

She put her head on his shoulder, left it there for a brief moment, and then jerked it away quickly. "Thanks," she said softly.

"Listen, there really isn't much to do, snowed in like we are, but would you like to walk around the hotel a bit? There are places you haven't seen. The *Kegelbahn*, and the --"

"The what?"

"*Kegelbahn*. It's kind of like bowling, except the ball and the pins are smaller. And there is a nice little gift shop that's not full of touristy souvenirs. If it's open, there is also a small clothing boutique, mostly ski clothes, but they do have a few other things. How about it? No more bad thoughts?"

"I guess. If you want."

"No, no, if you want."

"Okay, but don't feel like you have to cheer me up."

"I won't, but I would like to stroll around some. Our room is probably being cleaned right now anyway." He got up and held out his hand, which she took; after helping her up, he hooked her arm in his as they walked down a hallway studded with deer antlers.

"I'm glad you didn't use that gun anymore. Life is so precious, I don't see how anyone can kill for sport, just take it and just snuff it out." She stopped, took his hand and placed it on the upper right side of her swollen belly. "Do you feel it?"

He certainly could feel it, a rippling movement beneath her flesh, then a sudden thud, followed by another.

"That's what matters. The girls I live with all think I'm crazy for having this baby, but I never once thought of not having it." Her hand still rested on his, pressed against the baby's active feet and legs that played beneath it. "I just want the life I'm carrying to have a chance, is all. Just a chance."

"I'm sure it will, Jenny. You are going to be a good mother, I can tell."

"I hope so. I really hope so."

"I know so." He took his hand away, looped her arm back through his and led her on down the hall toward the gift shop.

"Oh, how nice."

It was small, but artfully arranged with a real variety of wood carvings, jewelry, hand-crafted pottery, lovely crystal made in the area, and even a few traditional beer steins. They separated and meandered, he watching her take joy in every small item, lifting a dark blue pitcher, holding it up so its glaze caught the light, a Madonna and Child carved with delicate features, the infant at its mother's breast, Oberammergau stamped on its base, and then she was drawn to the glass case filled with jewelry, necklaces, earrings, bracelets, many made of native stones and silver still mined in the region.

He watched her more than he looked at the gifts. *"Ich sehe mich nur um,"* he thought to himself, one of the first German phrases he had learned years ago, "I'm just looking." He was just looking, wasn't he? Could there be any more to it than that? She took such child-like joy in everything, the smallest things, and suddenly, long forgotten lines from Browning's "My Last Duchess" came to mind, the joy from the gift of a bough of cherries or in the dropping of the daylight in the west. He certainly hoped that she would find a better end, and then he saw that she was crying again.

"What is it?"

"Nothing," she said, shaking her head, turning away from him.

"We aren't married, remember?" He tried to tease, but to no effect.

"I know . . . I know, and I'm not . . ." she began, turning toward him, but then stopped and turned back away. "You really don't want to hear it."

"How do you know I don't? I want to hear anything you want to tell me."

"Maybe I just don't want to tell it then."

"That's a different matter, then, but I can't imagine not wanting to hear everything about you."

She took a deep breath, and turned back toward him. "I was just looking at the locket in the case, the silver one." She pointed to a small, heart-shaped locket with fine engraved scrollwork. "I think I had one like that when I was little," she said quickly, letting the air out of her lungs in a rush.

"Think?"

63

"Yeah. I have this memory, clear as anything, of this silver locket shaped like a heart, and I'm holding it open and inside is the picture of a woman with long, dark hair. That image just comes to me sometimes out of the blue. It makes me happy at first, but then I always feel sad afterward. I don't really know if I ever had a locket like that, and I don't know who the woman is. I used to think it was maybe my mom, but now I'm not sure -- I'm not even sure about the locket."

"Is your mother still living?" And just as soon as he had asked, he remembered what she had told him earlier.

"I never knew my parents, Mr. Leiden. I don't know where I come from. I have absolutely no memories before the age of seven or so. It's just a blank. I remember being in this home, an orphanage, I guess. It was horrible. Not that I was mistreated, or anything, I just remember how horribly alone I felt. There were other kids, but for some reason, I didn't know any of them. I think I had the locket then, but I could be mistaken."

"God, Jenny, that's terrible."

"Yeah, for a little kid it was. Then I just moved from foster home to foster home. I think they thought I was autistic or retarded or something, because I never used to talk. I could, I just didn't. I discovered that if you didn't talk, people left you alone, and for whatever reason, that's what I wanted, to be left alone."

"I see why there were no memorable Christmases, Jenny. I didn't understand. I'm so sorry."

"I do remember one Christmas, though. I stood in line with lots of other kids waiting to see Santa at some fire station. Everybody was so excited when he came rolling up in a bright red fire truck, sirens blaring away. Everybody except me. I felt humiliated. I knew that the only reason I was there was because I didn't have a family. Anyway, I stood in line because my foster mother made me, but when I finally got up to the front, they had run out of presents. I remember her saying, 'Well, you can't expect Santa to make every kid happy, can you? There's just too damned many kids in the world.' There you have it, Mr. Leiden, my most memorable Christmas."

Huge tears streamed down her face, and she tried to brush them away with her fingertips. He took her in his arms and held her gently until she had stopped crying. "I won't have my baby go through what I went through. I'll do anything to make sure that doesn't happen. Anything," she said in a harsh whisper edged with an anger that he fully understood.

"Life isn't very fair sometimes, Jenny. Sounds like you've had more than your share of unhappiness." He took out his handkerchief and dabbed at her wet cheeks. "Want to check out the clothes?" he asked, nodding to a doorway from the gift shop.

"I guess so."

He had been right, most of the things in the shop were ski clothes, pants and tops, shells, thick, down filled parkas. "I don't think I'm going to be doing any skiing," she said with an ambiguous laugh.

"Maybe not, but you do need a warm coat. That windbreaker of yours just wont do." He took a blue quilted parka from the rack, turned her around and held the shoulders of the coat up across the back of her own. "That looks about right. The color okay?"

"You know I can't buy that."

"That's right, but I can." He made her try on the coat, even though she didn't zip it up.

"I can't let you do this, Mr. Leiden. You've done too much already."

"Erik. Erik. Come on, Jenny, if we're going to be friends, call me Erik. 'Mr. Leiden' makes me sound about a hundred years old. Don't remind me that I'm almost halfway there."

"I'll try . . . Erik, but you really can't buy this for me. I have no way to repay you."

"It's a matter of self-interest, Jenny. If you wear that windbreaker, you're going to catch your death of cold. Then I'll feel guilty as hell, and you know it. So just let me off the hook, okay? It's just a coat," he said, but she noticed that he held the price tag tightly in his closed fist.

"You're impossible, do you know that?"

"I try to be."

They took the coat back to the front desk, and Frau Holzman added its cost to his bill. "*Sie ist eine schöne Dame, Herr Leiden. Ist sie nicht etwas ganz Besonderes?*"

Yes, she was beautiful, but did Frau Holzman think there was something between them? "For me?" he asked.

"Naturally, for you. You seem so very happy this visit, if I can say," she said with a wink of a bright blue eye. "*Ihre Augen ...* they are beaming."

No, he assured her, she was not someone special, only an accidental traveling companion. But she was right, wasn't she? He was happy. Happier than he had been for a long time. And maybe his eyes were sparkling. After all, rather than spending his Christmas alone as he had expected to do, Jenny had unexpectedly filled the emptiness. What was so bad about that?

"What did she say," Jenny wanted to know. "It was about me, wasn't it?"

"Well, if you must know, she said you were very pretty."

"Really?"

"Of course, 'really'."

"That's all?"

"Isn't that enough?

"Yes," she said. "Quite enough." With one arm in his and her new coat in the other, they walked back down the hall toward the stairs, her with a new bounce in her step, him hoping that their room would have been made up by the time they got back to it.

Once inside, she put on her coat, zipped it up, and twirled around. It was pretty snug around the middle, he noticed, but it was okay. "I love it," she said. "Thank you, thank you, thank you." She came to him, tiptoed and gave him a quick kiss on the cheek. "At this very moment, I feel like the luckiest girl in the whole world."

"I'm glad that you like it, but I'm afraid I've got some bad news for you. I hope you don't mind, but I asked Frau Holzman to check out your Regensburg address. I didn't say anything about you, though."

"Just now?"

"No, no, this morning when I went down for coffee. I asked her if she knew the city, and she said she didn't know it well, but one of her best friends lives there. So she called her and checked out the address. No such place, Jenny. Even the city code is wrong."

"I was afraid of that," she said, sitting down on the side of the bed as if she were deflating, shaking her head. "Shit! Shit! Shit! That bastard!"

"It was kind of a long shot anyway, wasn't it?"

"Maybe to you, but it was the only shot me and my baby had. Don't you see that? I told you, I'll do anything for the sake of my baby, and I will."

He expected her to break into tears, but she didn't. Finally she asked him, "Would you mind if I was by myself for a while? I know it's your room and all, but I'd just like to be alone, if I could."

"Sure. Whatever you want." He walked toward the door, and then stopped. "Any man who would leave you, Jenny Heilman, is for sure a bastard, but he also has to be an absolute fool. I'll be downstairs. You come and find me when . . . if you want company." He closed the door quietly behind him.

7

He wandered aimlessly around the hotel, a hotel he knew too well for wandering. He went down into the lowest level and watched several older couples using the *Kegelbahn* for a while, their boisterous enthusiasm exposing the lie of the quiet German. Men and women, they all drank heartily from tall glasses of pale pilsner. He went to the small exercise room, climbed on a stationary bike and rode idly for a while, wondering how such a sweet girl could have had such rotten luck in life. He thought of his own daughter, how fortunate she had been. Some time later, he found himself at the hotel entrance, pushing his way out into the entryway. The chill hit him right away, and then he pushed out into the real cold.

Snow still fell, but at least the wind was little more than a chilly whisper. His skin prickled, and he stuck his hands in his pockets. What the hell was he doing standing there? He didn't know, yet he didn't move. The narrow road that ran through the village had disappeared, but he followed the way that it should have taken up to the small church, its onion dome dark beneath its cap of snow. Funny, all the times he had been there, and he had never gone inside. He supposed he had seen too many baroque churches in his day.

"What are you doing?"

"What?" She had startled him.

"What are you doing standing out here in the cold?"

"Musing. Just musing."

"You'll be the one to catch your death of cold. Then where'll I be?"

"Where ever you are, you're going to be just fine, Jenny. I know it. What ever happens, you're going to make it."

"Well, come back in, because I'm getting cold, and I . . . I missed you."

They went back in and sat by the fireplace for a while, neither of them saying anything. He didn't know what to say, and she didn't help him. He just wanted to know that she was okay, but he didn't want to ask.

And then as if reading his mind, she said, "Yes, I'm fine. Get that fatherly look of concern off your face. You're right, I'm going to be okay, no matter what. I'm a big girl."

Not so big, he thought, but he did think that she would be okay, or maybe he just hoped that she would be. That was an unsettling difference, and he knew it. Finally he said, "See that sign over there, with the musical notes on it?"

She nodded.

"It says that after dinner tonight there is going to be a dance. Do you have your dancing shoes with you?"

"You've got to be kidding. These sensible things are the only ones I have," she said, sticking her legs straight out in front of her and knocking her combat boots together. "Anyway, I don't know how to dance, really. I don't ever remember being at a dance."

"That's okay, I'm not much of a dancer either. Used to drive my wife crazy. She was always trying to teach me, but she didn't have much patience, most often giving up in a huff. Maybe I really do have two left feet like she said. Hey, it's almost lunch time. I feel like a nice bowl of soup. How about you?"

"Oh yes, soup sounds good. And I'll bet Herr Holzman makes wonderful soup, right?"

"How did you know?" he said with a smile. "It's all in reducing the stock, having patience. Americans just don't have the patience for good soup. And fresh ingredients, popped in

69

at just the right time. Soup has to be tended to, not just turned on and left to cook. What are you grinning at?"

"You. I love the way you get excited about food, and wine and beer. You really care about things like that. I don't know anyone who gives a damn about such things. It's just nice that you do. I wish I knew half of what you do."

"You know your own things, Jenny. Don't forget that?"

"Well, I'd like to forget some of the things I know, and you probably wouldn't like me at all if you knew some of the things about me."

"I don't believe that for a minute, Jenny. But you don't have to tell me anything, you know. Not a thing."

"Yeah, I know that, but will you tell me something? No, no, you don't even really have to tell me," she said, shaking her dark bobbed head. "I'm just wondering about something."

"If I can, but let's do it over lunch, okay?"

He got up, helped her, and they walked toward the dining room, already half filled with guests. The girl who had served them coffee and camomile tea at breakfast took their order at lunch.

"So what are we having?" she asked. "I didn't understand a word."

"It's called *Rindfleischsuppe mit Flädle*. It's like a rich beef broth with small pieces of beef and thin strips of cut up pancake. Herr Holzman even makes his with bone marrow. It sounds rather dull, I know, but it's really quite good, and it might even be good for you, who knows?"

When the girl returned, she carried a large tray with a blue and white soup tureen and two large bowls. The young waitress served her first and then him. *"Guten Appetit,"* she said, and left the tureen on the table.

"Oh, Erik, this is wonderful," Jenny said after her first spoonful. "I have to admit that it didn't sound so great when you described it. I'm glad she left the rest."

"I thought you would like it."

"I don't just like it. I love it."

"Okay, you shared some uncomfortable things this morning, what is it you want to know about me?" he asked her, wiping his mouth with his linen napkin.

"I hope it's not all that uncomfortable. I just wondered what you were really doing here all alone. I know you have a family, if not a wife. And it's Christmas time. Why aren't you with them, or them with you?"

"Ah, yes. Family? Why is it always a long story? But I'll try to make it brief. I've spent quite a bit of time in Germany over the past twenty years. I've always liked the country and the people, and the food and drink, you know about. You already know how much I've always liked Christmas. For years I dreamed of spending Christmas here with my family. A time or two, I even began to plan, but something always came up. It was never my wife's dream, by the way. Finally, six years ago, I thought it was really going to happen, and then on November 26th, my wife filed for divorce. Christmas in Germany shot to hell -- along with my life as I had known it."

"That must have been really hard."

"I guess it's all relative, Jenny. Compared to yours, my life has been a cake-walk."

"So what about now?"

"Well, this summer I told the kids -- not kids anymore, Ted is almost twenty-nine, Alec is twenty-seven, and Amanda is twenty-four -- anyway, I told them that I was spending this Christmas in Germany, come hell or high water, and I wanted them to come along. I would pick up their air-fare and room and board for a week. All they had to do was make it to the airport. Even though they all said they would come, I wouldn't have bet on it. Ted is, well, he's my son, but he's a cokehead. Lives up in Big Bear. Makes rocking horses and snorts coke. How's that for balance? And the rocking horses are for shit.

I really never expected him to come, but I thought the other two would for sure."

They ate their soup and hearty dark rye bread, and didn't talk for a long time. Finally he wiped his mouth with his napkin, and picked up again. "Alec told me in October that he was possibly changing jobs, and if he did, he wasn't sure how comfortable he would be asking for time off. And then Amanda informed me in late November that her current boyfriend -- there have been many, by the way -- expected her to spend Christmas with him in San Francisco. So, that's how I've ended up here all alone -- well, not exactly all alone," he said smiling at her. "That's how I've ended up here."

"I know it must have been a real bummer, but at least you didn't let that stop you. You came anyway. I think that's neat. And besides, I wouldn't have met you if you hadn't come, and meeting you has been something really special for me. I know for you I'm just some goofy, knocked up ding-bat, but irregardless of what you think about me, you've treated me like a real person. I'll never forget you for that. Never."

"I think lots of things about you, Jenny, but I've never thought of you as a ding-bat or goofy. Knocked up? Well, pregnant, yes, but never knocked up."

She was smiling. "I remember the look on your face on the plane when you helped me with my bag. Come on, admit it. You thought I was kinda weird, didn't you?"

"I obviously didn't see you, Jenny. I just saw the rings and studs and what not."

"Yet you still helped me anyways, because you're a kind man."

"I keep telling you, check it out with my ex-wife. She could tell you stories, I'm sure."

"I don't need any stories. I've seen you in action."

"Not for twenty-four years you haven't."

"Long enough," she said, her lavender eyes firm and steady.

After lunch they returned to the room where she napped and he read. He was half-way through *The English Patient*, and identified with Caravaggio, thumbless and old, maimed but not enough so as to have excuses. She slept beside him, curled close, but not touching. She looked like a child, one of those Russian dolls, he thought, a child with a child inside. He reached out and touched her hair and was surprised. Though her hair was thick, it was ever so soft, almost like stroking ermine he thought as his fingers moved gently from crown to ear. She stirred and he lifted his hand away. She deserved more than she had gotten in life, and he regretted that he couldn't give her more. But he wasn't a miracle worker. He was pretty sure that Regensburg was a dead end, but she was right. What else did she have?

It didn't seem that it would matter though, because the snowfall had increased and the wind had picked up. It shuddered the outer panes of the double-glazed windows, but something deep inside him found it satisfying. His inner weather seemed strangely fine.

She had dressed for dinner in a white, shapeless shift that fell to her ankles, but on her it looked fine, even if the combat boots spoiled the entire effect. He could ignore that. They began with a somewhat spicy goulash soup, and she was concerned about heartburn, but he promised her he had lots of antacid back in the room. He ordered a pork tenderloin in a green sauce with potato croquets for himself, and for her, he had gone into the kitchen and asked Torsten and Herr Holzman to prepare a flame-grilled chicken breast with a lightly herbed yogurt sauce that she "ooood" and "aaaahed" over during the course of the meal.

After dinner, dishes cleared away, him drinking his favorite *Kirschbrand* and her a mineral water with lemon, she said that she wanted him to know something. It might change the way he thought about her, but she needed to tell him anyway.

"Okay, Jenny, out with the deep dark secrets."

"Not so deep, but I don't know how dark. You'll have to figure that out for yourself. I think I told you I left school at sixteen. I hated school. Schools, really. I never stayed at any one school long enough to meet anyone or make any real friends. I moved from foster home to foster home, you know, and along with that went moving from school to school. So, I quit when I was sixteen. That sort of went along with getting thrown out of my last foster home. The man was a really creepy guy, always looking at me, touching me, never openly sexual like, you know, but I knew that lecher's look, and I hated it. One night I woke up and there he is in my bed, naked, trying to shove his cock up between my legs. I screamed like bloody hell, and his wife comes running in yelling at me. At *me*, mind you, at me. 'You little whore! I knew it, you little whore!' she kept yelling. And told me to get my fuckin' ass out of her house and never come back. So I did, and I never went back to the Children's Protective Services office either. Lot of fuckin' protection they'd given me, huh? Then I lived on the streets in Hollywood for a long time." She stopped and took a drink of her mineral water.

He saw how difficult this was for her. "You don't have to tell me any of this, Jenny. Nothing you can tell me will change how I see you or feel about you. Don't you know that by now?"

"Maybe I need to tell it for me, Erik. You're the only person in my whole life who has treated me the way you do. Like a human being. Like you actually care about me. About what's going on inside of me. I know I probably haven't helped that. The way I dress and make up. It's all pretty much a mask, though. People think they know exactly who and what I am by the way I look. It makes everything real simple. I don't have to expose myself, and they don't have to try and figure out who I am. Protection both ways, I guess. All I ever wanted to do most of my life was to survive, to be left alone and just survive. But now, for the first time, I know that I want something more."

"We all wear masks of one kind or another, Jenny. Even me."

"If you wear a mask, Erik Leiden, it's pretty damned transparent." She managed a smile along with her confidence.

"Maybe not as transparent as you think."

"So. I lived on the streets for a long time, like I said, but I want you to know that I never tricked."

"Tricked?"

"Yeah, I never sold myself . . . you know . . . for sex. I panhandled, begged, scammed, all that crap, but I never hooked. I don't really know why, but I wanted you to know that about me. I did other stuff, though, stuff I'm not proud of. I danced topless off and on, mostly off. 'Not enough tit,' they'd always say, but it never stopped them from trying to fuck me. Then about the third month, poof, my breasts started to swell up. Then I got lots of work for a while and saved my money, but that didn't last too long. I started to show just when I was working regular."

He was speechless. How was he supposed to respond to all that? All he could say was, "God, Jenny, I'm so sorry you had to do that," and shake his head.

"I think it made me stronger, though. That's good, because I have to be strong for my baby. I don't think I could have come all this way if I hadn't gone through all that. I read some place that Hemingway said we are stronger in the broken places. I like that. I figure I'm pretty much broken all over, so maybe I'll be stronger all over."

75

"I'm sure you will be, Jen. I'm sure you will be." He didn't think that he would have the courage to have gone through all that and be half the person she was. What if he hadn't stopped in the airport? He would never have had the opportunity to see beneath the mask.

"I like that."

"Like what?"

"You called me 'Jen'. Nobody's ever called me that before."

Before he could say anything, Frau Holzman entered the dining room and explained that even though all the band members couldn't make it, they were going to begin the music with those that had. On a raised platform in the corner were a youngish portable keyboard player wearing black pants, white shirt, and a red vest, an older sax player, and an even old man with an accordion, and finally a short, chubby, red-cheeked bass player, all dressed the same. Some combo, he thought to himself, but he supposed they were lucky to have any of the members make it through the snow.

After a few polkas, they played a slow number, and he leaned across the table. "Would you like to dance?"

"You still want to dance with me?"

"Nobody else." He stood up and reached out his hand.

"I wasn't lying. I really don't know how to dance. Not this kind of dancing, anyway."

"We'll just move around then. We'll pretend we're dancing, how's that?"

"Okay." She gave him a crooked little grin.

He led her into the middle of the dining room, and they began to move in time with the music, managed to avoid the other couples on the floor, and forgot that they couldn't dance.

"Is it awkward for you?" she wanted to know.

"What?"

"This great bulge between us."

"It's fine. Your little chaperone. I have to keep my distance," he said, slowly becoming aware of even greater distances that would have to be kept between them.

She smiled up at him and managed to lean far enough to put her head on his shoulder. Before they knew it, people were romping around them in a polka, and they returned to their table. They sat out the fast, galloping songs, and danced to the slow, learning to fit together, he turning left, she right, moving as one, and by the time the band was saying *auf Wiedersehen*, they had become comfortable with one another.

"Oh look," he said, patting her belly, "You're turning into a pumpkin. I'd better get you home."

She playfully slapped his shoulder. "Don't forget, these aren't glass slippers I'm wearing, mister. They can kick some butt."

"I give."

"Good, 'cause I'm really tired -- I've had a wonderful time, though. Thank you so much. Now I'm ready for bed."

"We'll save the coach ride for another night then."

Back in the room she said, "You don't mind if I sleep in the bed?"

"You know I don't. I offered it from the beginning. I just didn't want you to feel uncomfortable."

"Not anymore. Not with you." She went into the bathroom, and when she came out she was wearing her long, tented tee-shirt. She turned back the comforter and climbed into bed.

He went into the bathroom, took off his clothes and put on his pajamas. "Night, Jen. Sleep tight," he said as he came back and got into his side of the bed.

"Good night, Erik. Thanks for everything, and especially for dancing with me, the only pregnant woman at the ball."

"Ah, but she was my pregnant woman," he responded, half wishing that it were true, and then reached over and patted her on the shoulder. "You two sleep well."

"*Bis morgen.*"

"*Ja, bis morgen, mein Schatz.*"

"And what does that mean, *mein Schatz?*"

"Oh, just . . . something like . . . little one," he lied only a little.

She was a treasure, wasn't she, but one that he could never keep. Sleep didn't come as easily as it had the night before, but eventually it did come, hard and fitful.

8

"No," she cried, "Not my baby! Please! Please! Stop. Help! Somebody help me!" She thrashed and flailed beside him.

"Jenny! Jenny! Wake up. You're having a dream. It's just a dream." He reached out to still her, then held her tightly in his arms. "Just a bad dream, Jenny."

"Oh, Erik, Erik, it's horrible. Always the same . . . they're taking my baby . . . taking it . . . telling me I'm not fit to be a mother . . . they have to put it in a home."

She trembled uncontrollably in his arms, clutched at him as if he alone could save her. "Shhhhh, Jenny, it isn't real, none of it. Hush, Jen, hush. I'm here. Right here."

"It's always the same, over and over, the same dream. I hate it. I hate it!"

"Just remember . . . it's a dream, honey . . . not real . . . can't hurt you," words he had used so many times with his own daughter when she had been small. He cradled her head in his hand, held it against his face, whispered into her ear, his lips brushing the warm contours of her flesh. "Can't hurt you. Ever."

The trembling lessened, and when she had been still for a long time, he said, "All right now?" She nodded her head against his face. "Want to try to sleep again?" Again she nodded, but when he tried to release her, she clutched him to her. "Hold me, please. Just till I fall asleep. Please, hold me."

He lay beside her, his arms around her, the gap between the two mattresses beneath him. A small discomfort, he thought, if it would bring her peace. She lay with her head cradled in the crook of shoulder and arm. Surprisingly, she was breathing easily within minutes, and he could feel the muscles of her body slowly relax beside him. Long after his arm had fallen asleep, tingling from the loss of circulation, he held her still, and was suddenly aware that he wished he could go on holding her forever, but he knew that that could never be, would never be. He willed away the numbness in his arm and embraced the moment that he had, the warmth of her sleeping form.

Some time later in the night he woke to see her standing at the window, drapes parted, a strange light slicing into the room. "What is it? Bad dream again?" He was still groggy, and she looked absolutely ethereal standing in the glow of that strange luminescence.

"No," she said almost inaudibly.

He raised himself on one elbow. "What are you doing?"

"I'm watching a poem?"

"A poem?"

"Yes, I think I'm looking at a poem, 'the moon on the breast of the new fallen snow.' Come to the window, Erik. It's beautiful . . . beautiful."

He got out of bed and went to her. Out the window a full moon in a cloudless sky cast its light over the snow-bound countryside, illuminating all with a silvery glow, even the quick-silver runnels down her cheeks.

"You're crying, Jen." He held her. It was becoming so easy to do, too easy. "Don't be sad."

"I'm not sad, silly. I'm happy, happy for the only time I can remember in my entire life. You've given me all this, Erik. I owe you so much."

"You don't owe me a thing, Jen. I'm just glad you're happy. I don't want you ever to feel that you owe me anything."

"This is like my first Christmas. And to be having it with you in Germany, isn't that something?"

"Yes, it's really something." He hugged her tighter than he should have, and wanted desperately to kiss her, but he knew that that was a step that he didn't dare take, for both their sakes. "You are something."

She leaned her head against his shoulder, and they stood at the window for a long time, until she finally kissed him on the cheek, turned away and said, "I'm going back to sleep and have a wonderful Christmas dream. I think you're going to be in it."

He stood at the window for some time longer, looking at the onion dome of the church glistening in the moonlight, counting houses almost covered by drifts along the village road, watching the silvery sentinels of fir guarding the flanks of the wintered hills, reminding him that there were still forbidden paths, ways that could not be traversed regardless of how enticing, more dangerous than the joy they seemed to promise.

While she slept, her breathing a now familiar metronome of her wellbeing, he lay bathed in the cold moonlight, wondering for the first time in nearly two days if coming here hadn't been a huge mistake after all. But here he was, bound by circumstance to the person who had given him more happiness in a few short days than he had know in the last six years, but knowing full well that it was a happiness that would have to end.

Sometime just before dawn he fell into a dark, unwholesome sleep.

"Wake up, Erik. Wake up. The sun is out. The storm is over. Get up."

He turned back the comforter and looked at her with what felt like bloodshot eyes. "Jesus, what time is it?" Then he

81

took her in. She stood there holding a tray with his coffee and her herbal tea.

"Coffee in bed, my lord."

"Jesus, give me a sec, Jenny."

"Sure," she put the tray down on the desk. "Everything okay?"

"Yes, everything's fine. Just having trouble waking up, I guess." He went to the bathroom, washed his face, brushed his teeth and combed his hair. Back in the room, she sat on the loveseat, legs curled beneath her, too much of one slim thigh and curve of buttock showing, sipping her tea.

"I guess I shouldn't have woken you up. It was just so exciting to see the sun. I should've let you sleep. I'm sorry."

"No, that's okay." His musings of last night had spilled over into the morning. He had no reason to take it out on her. It wasn't her fault. If anyone was to blame for his predicament, it was he himself and his own foolishness. He was too old for this. It was a young man's disease, and she just happened to have gotten caught in his anachronistic affliction. She was an innocent, an innocent who had lived much more than he in many respects, but an innocent none the less.

He poured a cup of coffee from the small silver server, the hot milk, and finally added sugar and stirred, looking at her all the while. Then he became aware that he was standing there in his pajamas, half hard and old, old, so old. What he wouldn't have given to be half his age. Hell, maybe even shaving off ten years would have been enough.

"You sure you're okay? I feel like I've done something wrong." She chewed gently at the corner of her mouth. "We're not married, you know," she said, but there was no smile.

"Right, Jen, right, and you haven't done a thing, kiddo," he said, got into his robe, walked over and gave her a kiss on the soft, dark crown of her fragrant head. "Never."

"Good. I'd never do anything I thought would make you unhappy."

"And you haven't. Thanks for the coffee. I think that's all I needed. I'm a bit of a coffee addict, as you've probably noticed. Can't get started in the morning without it. See, you've resuscitated me. I'm alive again." He bent and kissed her head again, intoxicated by the smell of her shampooed hair. He hoped that his mask wasn't too transparent, for his words hadn't been far from the truth. She just didn't know it. "Maybe they'll get the car out if the storm is over. Then we'll get you to Regensburg."

"I've thought about that a lot, Erik, and it's not important any more. If he didn't want me, he sure isn't going to want my baby. We're just going to have to make it on our own. Just me and my baby. I wouldn't want to be with someone who really didn't want me anyway. Obviously he didn't. I just wanted to believe that he did. I guess I needed to believe that. But believing isn't enough, is it?"

"No, Jen, I suppose not." He felt as if something deep inside of him were buckling, cracking, fissuring. He couldn't tell if something new was forming or whether something old was collapsing. He just knew that he had to sit down, had to still the hand that held his coffee cup, but most importantly, had to quiet his fibrillating heart.

They were both strangely quiet at breakfast, in contrast to the other guests who seemed to be supercharged by the sunlight that flooded through the tall, frosty windows of the dining room. He had little more than coffee and she played with more than ate her yogurt, twirling the small spoon around and around in the creamy mixed berry culture.

"Happy Christmas Eve," he said, finally breaking the brittle silence between them.

"Happy Christmas Eve," she returned, eyes fixed on a spoon full of yogurt.

"Did you know that the Germans exchange gifts on Christmas Eve? *Christkindlnacht* or *Heiligabend*. The night of the Christ Child. They really celebrate Christmas in one way or another from the first of December, what with Advent and all, but the real high season falls between the twenty-fourth of December and the sixth of January, Epiphany."

"I like that," she said. "Is that how long you're here for, then?"

"God no. I leave on the twenty-sixth. I have to be back in L.A. on the 27th for an important meeting. A small chain of wine shops wants to merge with my little one shop organization. They have the money, but little expertise, while I have the expertise, but little money. But back to Christmas, I suppose it's that German dedication to the season that brings me here in the first place. These folks really do Christmas right."

"Will you tell me something?"

"If I can."

"I told you I was ignorant. I don't really know what Epiphany is. I know the word, but I never understood it."

"In Germany it's called *Dreikönigstag*, The Three King's Day. The Magi, you know."

"'We Three Kings of Orient Are'?"

"The very same."

"And that's the name of the hotel, The Three Kings?"

"Right again."

"That's nice. And the Magi come to the the inn where the baby Jesus is, right? But what's Epiphany?"

"Well, for the Church, I guess, it's the realization that this baby isn't just any baby, but it is the Christ Child, the Messiah, The King of the Jews, the Savior, or whatever."

"You know Joyce?"

"Joyce?"

"Yeah, the writer."

"Oh, yes, James Joyce. I read him some in college, but I was never a great fan, I'm afraid."

"Well, he was on this list I had, and I got a book, the artist one, and I really did try to read it, but I didn't understand it very much. I liked the way he used words, though, the way he described that girl on the beach with the seaweed around her leg and all, but as I said, I didn't understand him. So I looked him up in an encyclopedia about modern literature and all, and I remember it said that he used these epiphanies all the time. Is that the same thing?"

"Jen, you're amazing. And yes and no, I suppose is the answer. The idea is the same, so you're right again. I guess Joyce used it to suggest that there are common, ordinary events that trigger deeper understandings, revelations of a kind, of some deeper meaning. Kind of an 'ah ha!' experience. But it's the same idea, just more general, not specifically religious. But I have to confess something, too. I tried to read *Ulysses*, and I didn't understand lots of it, so don't think you're dumb for not getting all of Joyce. Many of us don't."

"Mmmm, you're sweet. Thank you," she managed, her mouth half full of yogurt. And then brightening, "I want to go outside today. I want to play in the snow. I've never played in the snow, Erik, and I think I should. Will you come with me? If you leave on the 26th, we only have two more days together, right?"

"Of course I'll come with you, but just because the sun is shining doesn't mean that it's warm out. You need to dress warm."

"Yeah."

"Why don't you go on back to the room. I've got some odds and ends to take care of, a call or two to make. I'll meet you back in the room when I'm through, and then we'll go out for a while. Okay?"

"Good, I'll try and find my warmest clothes, but I really don't have anything much. I'm pure southern California, I guess."

"In a bit, then."

They parted, she heading down the hall toward the stairs, he in the direction of the gift shop and ski boutique.

When he entered the room, he found her sitting on the edge of the bed, her denim duffle between her feet. She had been crying, but was no longer.

"I don't have anything warm. Just my coat -- your coat."

"We'll fix that," he said, handing her a pair of thick, insulated ski pants and a top. "I hope they fit, especially over that pretty little tummy of yours."

Now the tears really came, her breath in ragged sobs. "Oh . . . god . . . I . . . I . . ." but she couldn't get the words out.

He sat down beside her on the bed, put an arm around her shoulders, and held her until the sobbing stopped. "Better hurry, the snow may melt before we get outside."

"For sure!" she said between snuffles. "Thank you. Thank you. Thank you. That's about all I ever have to say to you, isn't it? And every time I say it, I know I'll never be able to thank you enough."

"Well, it's more than enough. Let's see if those things fit."

He expected her to go into the bathroom, but instead she simply stood up, unbuttoned her dress, turned it back over her shoulders, and let it fall around her boots. She stood there a brief moment in bra and panties, simple cotton ones that hardly contained her full breasts, or her swollen belly. God but she was lovely, pregnant or not, she was absolutely beautiful, maybe even more so because of her pregnancy. Then she bent and picked up the ski pants, steadied herself by holding his shoulder as she slipped first one booted foot and then the other into the legs and then pulled them up. The Velcro belt and fly enabled her to cinch up the waist without an inch to spare. She beamed with the snug fit, and pulled the top on over her head.

"Do I look like a ski-bunny?"

"I'd better not tell you what you look like."

"Poooh," she said, wrinkling her nose and frowning.

"Here, these will have to do. The smallest they had," he said, pulling a pair of gloves out of his back pocket. "Let me get my coat, and we'll make a snowman."

"You're too good to me," she said, accepting the gloves, holding them against her cheek, then kissing them.

But he knew that he could never be good enough.

"I want to make angels, though," she said. "I've always wanted to make angels, but I've never been in the snow before."

"Then we'll make angels," he said, helping her on with her coat, and then taking her hand.

Outside they were not the only ones to find the sun, as old and young alike waded through the thick build-up, the village children shouting and squealing as they thrashed around, free from the confines of their homes for the first time in several days.

"Ooooh, it is cold, isn't it?" she said.

"Yes, so we shouldn't stay out too long." He helped her on with her gloves, and then put on his own. "Weather like this can be very deceptive." And then they high-stepped their way around the hotel until they found relative quiet and unspoiled white. Through a snow-clogged lane they could see the small church.

"Look at the sun on the onion dome, Erik." Light seemed to explode from the snow-clad tower, a small nova of shimmering fire. "Are you a believer?" she asked him suddenly.

"I used to be," was all he said.

"I wish I believed more. Especially right now, right here. Is the church nice inside?"

"Would you believe I've never been inside, Jen. I imagine it might be though. They took their churches seriously back then, even the small, out of the way ones."

"Can we go in?"

"I don't know if it's open -- usually Catholic churches are, but in this weather, I don't know. If you are up to it, though, we could go to Midnight Mass tonight? I'm sure they'll heat the church for that."

"Oh, could we? I'd love that. I've never been to Midnight Mass. What a Christmas, Erik. It's like my very first one, thanks to you." She squeezed his hand. "Sometimes I have to pinch myself. I'm afraid I'm going to wake up and you'll be gone, I'll discover this has all been a dream."

Well, in two days he would be gone, wouldn't he, and he sure didn't want to think about what might happen to her after that. It felt too good standing there holding her hand, looking down the snowy lane at the little parish church, its dome a small bright sun unto itself. What did all those poems he had read in college say, *carpe diem*? Yes, he would seize the day. Wasn't he standing there watching the "cherry hung with snow" as Housman had urged. Then she had flopped down into the snow and was moving her arms and legs.

"Make angels with me, Erik. Help me make angels."

Even though he felt rather foolish flinging his lanky frame down into the deep snow, he joined her, and side by side they carved out her angelic hopes beneath the winter sun, in singletons, in pairs, in small clusters, and soon the *Drei Könige* was graced by heavenly hosts, and somewhere along the way, he had stopped feeling foolish, drawn into her youthful exuberance and joy, her unencumbered appreciation of the moment, and then embraced the muffled thunder of his own beating heart and the heady roaring of his blood, and wishing desperately that he, too, could believe more.

"I've never been so happy," she said, holding tightly to his arm as they made their way back to the hotel entrance. "And we can really go to Midnight Mass?"

"Of course, if you are up to it and can stay awake that late."

"I'll take a nice long nap after lunch so I'll be wide awake."

For lunch they had eaten a delicious soup, really a stew, *Pichelsteiner*, full of cubed beef, pork and lamb, lots of quartered potatoes, large chunks of carrots, and a host of sliced onions, but the secret of the regional specialty, he had explained to her, was the marrow bones beneath it all. He had also told her that none of it was probably good for her, but she had been ravenous, and had eaten a full bowl.

Then, true to her word, she went upstairs to take a nap while he made a stop at the gift shop, another at the boutique, and finally one at the front desk where he had chatted with Frau Holzman. Finally he had stretched out in a comfortable chair near the fireplace and relaxed. He couldn't remember the last time he had felt so good, so satisfied, so at peace. The warmth of the fire and his own internal glow managed to keep at bay the pack of nagging questions that snapped and snarled just beyond the shadows.

9

The *Weihnachtsfest* was scheduled to begin at six-thirty, and they were both ready long before. "I'm sorry I don't have a nice dress to wear for you. You look so . . . so handsome."

He wore tan slacks, a darker brown sport coat with a pale yellow shirt and no tie. He sat in one of the chairs at the table, his long legs stretched out, crossed at the ankles, tasseled loafers on his feet.

"I'm sorry I couldn't find a dress for you, but the boutique doesn't cater to pregnant ladies, I'm afraid. But you look great, Jen. Hell, you would look great in a gunny sack."

"At least the slippers look better than my boots, don't they?"

"Not to criticize your footwear, but yes, they do." He had managed to find a pair of apres-ski slippers with ribbed rubber soles. They were dark and matched her black maternity shift.

"Isn't it time yet? Can't we go down now?"

"Boy, are we . . ." he had almost said "spoiled," but he had caught himself. Even in jest she was the least spoiled human being he had ever known, and he knew that all of his small niceties and attentions would never make up for her horrible deprivation. "Eager," he said, skipping that long thoughtful beat. "Well, then, if you really can't wait."

"I can't. I just can't. Christmas Eve at the *Drei Könige* with you. A feast! What could be better -- oh, yes, and Midnight Mass." She stood up and held out her hand to him. "And don't let me go to sleep. I mean it. I want to go, even if I'm sleepy. Just slap me awake and haul me off. I don't want to miss that. Promise?"

"Yes, I promise, but slapping's out."

"I knew it would be." She smirked at him. "I really can't wait," she said, taking his hand and pulling him up out of the chair.

The dining room was decorated, the lights dimmed, and a row of linen covered tables ran down the center of the room. At either end were countless *hors d'oeuvre, pâtés,* meats in aspic, on to salmon dumplings in Riesling sauce, raw and cured hams of all kinds, air dried beef and wild boar, on to the center where standing rib roasts tempted beside racks of lamb, and finally small suckling pigs flanked the Christmas goose at the very center of the table, its plump breast roasted a chestnut brown.

"This is incredible. I've never seen so much food, or food that looked so good." They held hands as they walked along the table, him naming every dish in German and explaining its ingredients, and what made it special or difficult to make. "*You* should be a chef," she said. "You know everything."

"No, I honestly have no desire to cook. My only desire is to eat. I just like to know what I'm eating, I guess."

Frau Holzman came into the dining room and saw them. "*Guten Abend,*" she said gayly. She was dressed in native costume, dark velvet skirt with bright applique and a lace apron. Tonight her white blouse displayed fine embroidery. "You are the first that arrives."

"I couldn't wait, Frau Holzman. I made him come down early."

"The early bird eats the vurm," she said.

"Not tonight. Everything looks wonderful," the girl said to her.

"And so do you, Miss Heilman," she said, all the while looking with a knowing grin and a sparkle in her eye. "I am happy that you can join us here. The *Drei Könige* is at this season . . . what is the word, not magic, *zauberhaft*."

"Magical," he helped her.

"I believe it, Frau Holzman. I've felt it ever since I arrived, even in that awful storm."

"*Hoffentlich bringt der Weihnachtsmann, was Sie wollen.* Enjoy your evening, please."

"What did she say?" Jenny wanted to know.

"She said that she hopes that the Christmasman brings you what you want. He's a little like Santa Claus, but not exactly." She didn't need to know that he had once had a much darker side than the American Santa Claus.

"Me too, then," she said softly. "Me too."

"*Wollen wir essen?*" he said, playfully patting her rear, then wishing he hadn't. That was an urge that didn't need indulging.

"I hope that means let's eat. As usual, I'm starving. And no diet tonight. I've lost all my will-power. I hope you understand, dear one." She patted her stomach gently.

And eat she did, especially the light, succulent salmon dumplings in the Riesling sauce. She even took a small sip of his German champagne from the Rheinhessen, and he told her about Dom Pérignon drinking stars, which she loved, and he told her where the other wines that they served along with the banquet were grown, about the vineyards.

"Once upon a time I could have told you about the families that grew the grapes, but that was a long time ago," he said, holding a glass of pale gold Franken wine from the village of Volkach east of Würzburg on the Main River. "I knew the man's father who made this wine, but I don't know the son." He took another sip, and was silent for some time.

"I used to spend so much time in the vineyards, with the growers, in little wine villages that most people have never heard of, looking for good wines at a good price. I helped prune the grape vines in winter . . . dress them in early spring . . . I helped pick the grapes . . . I helped crush and vat and bottle . . . I watched over them along with the *Winzer*, the wine grower, so I would better understand what I sold. I knew the rainfall in Piesport in any given year . . . the high and low temperatures in Johannisberg on the Rheingau. . . the names of wives and children, aunts and uncles. The wines I imported had histories and lives behind them, and I sold them with the same love with which the growers had made them. But that was a long, long time ago." He swirled the dry white wine around in the glass and finished it.

"It was a good time, though, wasn't it?"

"Yes, it was a very good time. But times change, don't they."

"Do they have to?"

"They say change is the only constant, don't they?"

She shrugged her shoulders and pushed her chair back. "I'll be right back."

"Are you okay?"

"I'm fine," she said, smiling at him strangely.

She returned shortly carrying a brightly wrapped package, green and red, and set it before him on the table. *"Frohe Weihnachten, mein Schatz,"* she said.

"Oooh, Jen, you didn't have to . . . you never . . . how did..." he was at a loss for words. Finally he said, *"Danke sehr, mein Herz,* and where did you learn your German?"

"Do you have to ask?" was all she said. "Open it. I hope you like it. Go on. Go on."

"Okay, patience." He untied the ribbon slowly, peeled off the clear tape, and opened the present carefully, exposing a long white box that closed at both ends. He opened one and pulled out a slender gift wrapped in white tissue paper. Inside he found the wood carving of Madonna and Child that she had been fingering in the gift shop. Its exquisite detail was arresting, the expression on the sacred mother's face, the baby at her breast, something much finer than the usual "school" produced carvings that one found throughout southern Germany. "Oh, Jen, she is lovely . . . you shouldn't have." How had she? She had no money!

"I want her to watch over you. I want her to take care of you. You have no idea how important you've become to me."

"Thank you, Jenny. Thank you." All he wanted to do was kiss her, hold her, but he knew he couldn't do that, so he slipped his hand into the pocket of his sport coat and pulled out a small square box covered with the same giftwrapping. He put it on the table and pushed it across to her.

"For me?"

"For you."

And she opened it just as carefully as he had opened his. The wrapping off, she lifted the lid off the small white box and found the silver, heart-shaped locket resting on a bed of cotton. The tears came suddenly, in a rush, so quick and hard that he thought that he had made a horrible mistake. Struggling to keep his balance, he said, "The silver comes from a mine a few miles from here, the Silberberg, just south of Bodenmais. I thought . . ." Hell, it didn't matter what he had thought. She sat clutching the box with both hands, head down, racked with sobbing.

"Hell, Jen, I'm sorry. I didn't mean to upset you. I thought it would make you happy."

She lifted her head, her lavender eyes even brighter from the tears. "Can't you see how happy you've made me?" Smiling through her tears, she took the locket and opened it.

"I know there isn't a photo of your mother, but --"

"I've got another photo in my head that goes there now, Erik." She snapped the locket shut, clutched it in one hand and held it between her breasts. "You are the most wonderful man."

"Then why are you still crying?"

"Because I want to kiss you so bad, and I don't know if you want me to, and I don't want to embarrass you in front of everybody. I've embarrassed you enough."

"There is nothing you could do to embarrass me, Jen. Nothing."

She got up from the table and walked around to him, leaned forward and kissed him softly on the lips, her own half-parted, warm, lingering long beyond what was good for either of them, her hand resting at the back of his neck.

Lifting her lips from his, she said, "I want to tell you . . . to tell you . . . that I . . . I . . . will never forget you. Thank you for being you, for being the person you are."

"Hush, Jen." He put his fingers to her lips.

"Will you put it on for me?"

"Yes, of course."

He stood up and she handed him the locket and chain. He slipped it around her long neck, and fastened the double clasp in back, where he had the strongest urge to kiss the olive skin just where it met the short dark hair of her bob, but he knew that there had been enough of kissing, no, more than enough. He couldn't allow himself the tumult of feelings that clamored for his attention. He couldn't allow himself to feel the scalding heat that flamed its way up his groin and belly, up into his heart and lungs. He felt as though he were hanging from a steep precipice by little more than his finger tips, giddy and reeling, about to slip into a head-long fall that would surely fracture more than his own frail ego.

"I love it," she said. "I absolutely adore it."

And I you, he couldn't say. And I you.

He had no idea where the evening had gone. Frau Holzman had spent some time with them at their table, appearing quite

95

smug and self-satisfied. She had hugged Jenny, even whispered conspiratorially into her ear. Later, even Herr Holzman had made an appearance, wishing them both a merry Christmas. They had sat by the fire in the lobby, saying little, but holding hands like sixteen-year-olds. Guests they had never spoken to greeted them and wished them well, and before they knew it, the church bell began to ring its chill muted call to Midnight Mass.

"You had better get bundled up. It's going to be really cold tonight, not like this morning."

"Okay, but you too."

There was a virtual line of people from the hotel making their way through the bright moonlight to Midnight Mass. They joined the procession, arm in arm, her back in her boots, him in walking shoes.

"I hope it's pretty inside," she said, her breath billowing against the cold.

"I'll bet it is, Jen. It just may surprise you."

As they entered the small church, the warmth was what hit them first, and then the smell of incense. In the vestibule sconced brass founts hung on either side of the central doors into the sanctuary.

"Is it okay if I cross myself? I'm not Catholic or anything."

"It's fine, Jen, just do what you feel like doing."

She pulled off her gloves and dipped the fingers of her right hand into the water, touched her forehead and each shoulder. "I don't even know if that's right."

"I imagine it's the intent that is important, Jen, not whether or not we do it right."

Once inside they could see the ornate baroque furnishings, and Jenny leaned against him, squeezing his gloved hand with her bare one. He pulled his free, took off his glove, and returned her hand to his. He wanted to feel her warm flesh, her heat, her life.

"You were right. It's so beautiful."

"The Germans have a word for such a thing," he said. *"Ein Kleinod,* a jewel, a gem, a small treasure. This is one if there ever was, Jen. It's lovely." The grand high altar stood in a Gothic alcove of salmon colored marble. Its own green base and spiraling, fluted pillars, topped by a curved lintel, housed a gilded Christ, one arm raised in benediction. On one side stood St. George with a lance and on the other St. Hubertus. On either side of the alcove separate altars of the same dark marble balanced the sides of the small bright church, one for the Virgin, the other for some saint he he didn't know. Votives and candles burned everywhere, and the soft light warmed as much as the fire that must have been set hours before.

"Thank you for this. I've never seen anything like it in my life. It's all so awesome. I love the gold, and the marble."

He didn't have the heart to tell her that most probably none of it was real, rather simply wood painted skillfully to resemble marble and gold. He had been told that his own great-grandfather had done such work.

Then he told her to look up, and she gasped; the barrel vaulted ceiling was home to a host of brilliant, white-robed angels, surrounded by billowing clouds, against a heaven of powder blue. "Angels, Erik, dozens of angels!"

"Just for you, Jen. Just for you."

"This place *is* magic, isn't it? The hotel, this church, all of it. Frau Holzman was right."

They took one of the back pews and participated in as much of the ritual as they could, neither being particularly religious, and neither Catholic, but they joined in when they knew the songs, carols old and new, and while the others sang in German, they sang in English, no one seeming to mind their joining in the *Weihnachtslieder,* all buoyed by the church's small organ, the pipes just above them in the choir loft, and her small, pure voice rose, quavered and pierced his heart when they sang "Silent Night."

"What is he saying?" she asked as an old priest delivered a brief homily, but he had to admit that he didn't understand the old man's Bavarian dialect, and then, much too soon for her, the service was over, and they were making their way back through the moonlit night to the festive glow of the hotel.

10

Still some distance from the hotel's walk way she stopped suddenly and clutched at his arm with surprising force. "Oh ... oh, God ... Oh, Erik ... Either I've peed myself, or my water just broke."

"But I thought you weren't due until --"

"I'm not. Oh, God, oooh, ooooh, God! I'm so sorry!" She bent over, holding his arm tightly.

"Nothing to be sorry about, Jen." He reached down and scooped her up into his arms.

"But I'm all wet!"

"Shush," he said, half kissing her, half silencing her. He hurried through the thick snow, thankful that the path to the church had been trampled on the way so that the going was somewhat easier. Now he had to make sure that he didn't slip and fall with his precious burden.

"You're going to be a mess," she cautioned him, her head on his shoulder.

"I'll live."

He hurried up the steps, careful for ice, and opened the door with the hand that held her under her back and shoulders. As they made their way through the interior doors, he called to Frau Holzman who stood behind the desk, "The baby! It's coming!" and hurried down the hall toward the stairs.

"*Ach, mein Gott!*" she cried. "Johann! Johann! Call the doctor. *Schnell! Schnell!* Freda, hot water and towels."

And then she was right behind him, stopping only long enough to open a standing cupboard just down the hall from their room.

"I'm so sorry, Erik. I'm spoiling everything, spoiling your Christmas."

"You haven't spoiled a thing, Jen. Not a thing."

"Wait," Frau Holzman said, and he stood holding the girl while she stripped off the bottom sheet and snapped out a thick rubber liner. She quickly returned the original and remade the bed, tucking in the edges and corners. "So! The doctor is to be called, but I don't know -- it is far and the roads are not yet clear. I will see to the hot water and towels and return."

"You'll be okay, Jen. Everything will be fine. Trust me. Even if the doctor doesn't get here, we can do this together. I was there for each of my children's births, and just last year, I delivered a baby in my own store, Jen, with the help of 911. Even got my three minutes of fame on local TV. I've done this. Now we can do it, Jen, we can do it together. Just relax. It's all going to be okay."

"I know. I trust you, Erik." She kissed him quickly on the lips. "Now put me down. I've already spoiled your clothes."

But as he bent and sat her feet just on the floor, she doubled over. "Oooooh. Mmmm," she moaned.

"A contraction?"

She nodded her head.

"Bad?"

Again she nodded.

"When did they start?"

"Off and on all day."

"Christ, Jen, why didn't you say something!"

"I didn't want to spoil it. It was all so perfect. This has been the best day of my life, Erik, I just couldn't let it end."

"It hasn't ended, Jen. We won't let it."

"I guess we'll see."

"We have to get you out of these wet things," he said, unzipping her coat, and turning it off over her shoulders, then pulling her top up over her head. "Can you stand?"

"I'm okay now. No pain."

"Good." Without a thought he pulled open the Velcro flap of her ski pants, separated the fly with a hiss, and finally pushed them over her hips and down her legs. "We have to, you know," he said, his hand in the waistband of her damp, stained panties.

"Go on, Erik. It's okay. I don't mind you seeing me. I trust you more than I thought I could ever trust another human being."

Without further hesitation he slid both hands inside the elastic band of her panties and turned them over the flare of her hips and down her slim legs. As he knelt at her feet, she stepped out of them. Instinctively he had turned his head away.

"Do I smell?" she wanted to know.

"No. Not in the least." He stood up and turned her slightly. "This too?"

"Go on."

He unhooked her simple cotton bra, and freed her breasts, again turning away from her slightly, but she circumvented his uneasiness, by moving with him. He couldn't avoid her high, full breasts, faint blue veins just beneath the smooth skin, nor the light brown areolas the size of half dollars and nipples distended like brown gumdrops.

"Why don't you want to look at me, Erik? I really don't ... ooooh!" again she doubled over with pain, biting her lower lip and squeezing his hand.

"I guess the baby's really coming, then."

"Afraid so."

"We've got to get you onto the bed, Jen." As he was helping her, Frau Holzman's quick rapping came from the door, and he covered her with the comforter.

"Come in."

"I have towels, and water, but *leider kein* . . . no doctor. He does not come until tomorrow. We have a . . . how do you say . . . no I have forgotten . . . *Hebamme*."

He shook his head.

"She helps at birth. I don't know the English."

"A midwife?"

"Yes, yes! In the next village."

"I don't know if there is time for that. I think we had better be prepared to deliver this baby ourselves."

Jenny had pulled the comforter over her nakedness when Frau Holzman had entered. "No midwife. Just you, Erik. Please. Just you. I don't want anyone to touch my baby but you. Promise me."

"No one will touch the baby, Jen, I swear it. I will deliver it. Just me."

"You? But how can that be?"

"That's okay, Frau Holzman. You just provide me with all I need, and I can manage. I need some sharp shears, some strong thread, some disinfectant if you have any, and just now, a basin of warm water, soap and a washcloth." He walked her to the door, and whispered to her just before she left, "And if you would just be close, just in case I need you."

"Of course, Herr Leiden. You are *wunderbar!*"

"No, just a man who wants the best for Jenny that I can give her."

"I am here if you need me, Herr Leiden."

"Thank you."

She came back in minutes with a basin of warm water, liquid antibacterial soap and a large fluffy washcloth.

"I will stand close by."

"Jen, we have to wash you before the baby comes."

"I know."

"Can you do it, or do you . . . do you want . . . me to?"

"I have no secrets from you, but I know I make you uncomfortable."

"It's just . . . I can't explain . . . Jen, I'll do whatever you want."

"You do it, then." She turned back the comforter and exposed herself to him again.

"Jenny, for whatever reason, I couldn't say it that first night when you came out of the bathroom from your shower wrapped in that towel, but you were beautiful, Jen, and you're beautiful now, even here like this. So beautiful, Jen."

He saw the tears gather in her eyes, and she shook her head side to side, jiggling her full, heavy breasts. "Yes you are," he said, and sat beside her on the bed, put the small basin between her legs, and soaked the washcloth in the warm water. He then wrung it out, squirted the liquid soap on it and then began to gently wash between the folds of her vagina, gently moving up and down between the puffy lips, then down beneath her sheath and lower, all the while looking into her lavender eyes, his fingers moving like those of a blind man over the braille of her body. Then he saw her grimace and felt her wince.

"Am I hurting you?"

"Anything but. How did you learn to be so gentle?"

His only answer was to rinse the cloth in the warm water, wring it slightly, then squirt more soap. Now he moved out from the pouty mouth of her sex and around, up into the fine, black pubic hair, down along her thighs.

"I wish it were all different," she said, her lavender-gray eyes moist. "I wish --" but another contraction cut her off.

He could see her stomach muscles spasm and contort, could see the baby being drawn down toward the place he washed. "Hang on, Jen. Breathe. Breathe. You can do it."

"If you help me."

"I'm going to be right here, honey. Don't you worry. Just breathe for me." By the time he had finished washing her,

103

Frau Holzman was at the door again, and he covered her with the thick eiderdown.

This time she carried a large stack of bath towels and hand towels. At the door stood Freda, one of the young serving girls, carrying two large kitchen pails with lids. Frau Holzman placed the towels on a chair and pulled it to the foot of the bed so they would be handy. On top of the towels was a bed sheet which she held out to him.

"This is for a covering, Herr Leiden. Better maybe than the comforter."

He took the sheet from her, carefully removed the thick eiderdown and replaced it, all the while keeping Jenny covered. "I can't thank you enough for all your help, Frau Holzman. We're sorry to inconvenience you in this way."

"No inconvenience, Herr Leiden. What greater gift than a Christmas child. It is the . . . magic of the *Drei Könige*," she said, winking at Jenny. And to him, "And here are kitchen shears, boiled. I think it is enough." The scissors were wrapped tightly in a white hand towel, and she placed them on the other side of the bed, and beside the shears, she laid a large spool of thick, dark thread. "Okay?" she asked.

"Perfect," he said, and then turned his attention to Jenny, whose stomach again twisted and knotted with its own will to bring her baby into the world. "Breathe, honey, breathe. No pushing yet."

"I am breathing . . . and I'm not . . . pushing," she said between clinched teeth.

"I know. You're doing fine. Just fine."

Frau Holzman brought in the kettles of hot water, and set them against the wall in the bathroom. "I am at the door should you need me."

"I'm sorry, Frau Holzman. You have been so nice to me. I just . . . I . . ."

"I understand, *mein Liebling*."

"I don't think she does," Jenny said as Frau Holzman left.

"Enough, Jen, she understands enough."

The girl just raised her eyebrows.

All was quiet as they both seemed to be waiting for the next contraction, but before it came, Jenny lifted herself on one elbow. "I think I have to pee, but I'm not sure. Everything down there feels weird."

"Can you get up?"

"Yes, but I want you to come with me." She threw off the sheet, swiveled her hips, and swung her legs off the edge of the bed until her feet touched the floor.

"Do you want my robe?"

"No, I'm fine. It'll be too hot for me. You don't like looking at me, do you? I'm too ugly like this, aren't I?"

"Christ, Jen, that isn't it at all. Don't you know that it's all I can do *not* to look at you. You're the most beautiful thing I've ever seen."

"And don't you know that I want you to look at me?"

"Now I'm looking, Jen. I can't help it. I'm looking."

"Good."

He helped her up and braced her with his hand beneath her forearm until they reached the bathroom door. He let go of her arm and said, "I'll be right here if you need me."

But she grabbed his arm as he tried to release her. "No, don't leave me. I don't want to be alone. I don't care if you see me pee. I don't care."

And so he stood beside her as she sat on the toilet and held his hand in both of hers, kissing the back of it, brushing her lips back and forth across the raised tendons that radiated from the wrist, all the while her water hissing into the bowl. When she was finished, she let go of his hand with one of hers, and with it pulled out sheet after sheet of paper from the roll, gathering it quickly in loops, and then wiped herself.

"Was that so bad?"

All he could do was smile in response and shake his head as he looked down into those alluring lavender eyes. He got her back in bed just as another contraction wrenched her body.

"Breathe. That's it. Just keep breathing. No pushing. Breathe."

She tried to smile through set teeth, and let the air suck in and out between them. Finally the muscles eased, and she relaxed.

"Good job, baby, good job."

"And just who are you complementing?" she wanted to know.

"What?"

"You said 'baby', and I just wondered which of us you were talking to."

He hadn't even heard himself, and was caught off guard with his own slippage. "Whomever was listening, I suppose." He wasn't sure what her smile meant. "Would you like me to rub your stomach? I know that sometimes helps."

"Oh, yes, if you wouldn't mind."

Mind? He wanted nothing more than to touch her, caress her, hold her. He slid his hand up under the sheet and gently rubbed and lightly massaged the taut flesh.

"Tell me about the early years."

"The early years?"

"Yes, when you were happy."

"What do you mean? Not with my wife?"

"No, silly, about when your business was just beginning, about how much you loved everything, the growers, the sites, the grapes themselves. Tell me about Willie Eisenreich and his vineyard on the Mosel so steep it's called the Goat Path. Tell me about how the mists hang over the Rhein in the early morning. About drinking the new, unfiltered wine and eating that onion thing on the Mosel. Tell me everything about when you were happy."

"*Zwiebelkuchen*, that's the onion thing, but that was a long time ago, Jen. And how do you know I was happy?"

"I see it in your eyes and hear it in your voice every time you talk about it. That was before you got 'too big', I think you said."

"Jesus, you were actually listening!" He continued to rub her smooth, taut skin.

"I listen to everything you say."

"Believe it or not, it all started with a glass of wine. I suppose I had drunk wine before, but it had never done anything for me. Sometime after I was married, we were at my parents-in-law's, and my wife's father opened a bottle of Chambolle-Musigny, and it was like paradise in a glass, Jen, deep, dark royal red, nose full of fruit, the scent of crushed currants and cigar boxes, but lacy, and the taste, a riot of sensation in the mouth and on the tongue, all caught up in a silky essence--yes, it was like drinking silk. I knew right then, the taste still lingering on my tongue, that my life's work would have something to do with that experience, I just didn't know exactly what that would be. Over time I learned that I had no desire to be a grower, just like I have no desire to be a chef. For a time I toyed with the idea of being a wine writer, I had been an English Major in college and wrote pretty well, but that kind of evaporated as I got more and more involved, wanting to have my hands on the subject rather than turn it into words."

He had to stop when the contractions came, holding her hand, comforting her as best he could, talking her through each excruciating series of spasms, but after each, she would beg him to continue. And so he told her about the early days, and in between the tastings in small cellars, the hectic joy of harvests in early autumn, the still times when they visited and drank and visited some more, of the many people that he used the informal *du* with instead of the formal *Sie*, but the contractions had begun to come more and more frequently, their intensity more wrenching and lasting longer.

He cautioned her to breathe, to pant, but not to push. The pushing would come later, he told her. And through it all his hand never left her belly, moved slowly in circular motions around and around, up the swell and down, from side to side, from top to bottom, brushing ever so lightly the fine dark hair that radiated from her pubis. He had never felt so alive in his entire life, nor so in love, but at the edges of the love stretched an expanse of sadness from which he turned away. He clung to the moment, knowing full well that this was a gestating love that could only come into the world stillborn.

By his watch it was three in the morning, and the contractions were coming every three or four minutes. "Jen, it's getting close, so I'm going to try and get you ready, okay."

"I've been ready for hours, Erik."

"I know, and you've been doing just fine." He folded a bath towel and was going to put it beneath her hips and buttocks, but when he removed the sheet he saw that her inner thighs and around and beneath her vagina were covered with bloody, amniotic discharge. Normal, he reminded himself, normal. "I need to sponge you off down here first, okay?"

"Yes."

He got the wash cloth and basin, discovering the water was cool. He hurried to the bathroom, poured it into the sink and got more warm water from one of the kitchen pails that was still warm.

"Talk to me," she said. "I don't want you to be away from me. I want to hear your voice."

"I'm right here, Jen, getting warm water. I'll be right back. One second. Just one," and he was already returning. "See."

"I'm sorry, Erik. I don't know why . . . I just . . . I need you to be with me."

"I am, sweet. I am. Right here."

He quickly cleaned her, and she was concerned about the blood, about the baby, but he assured her that it was all quite normal, everything was going well. Then he helped her lift her hips and positioned the folded towel beneath her.

"Stop! Another cramp. Hand! Hand!" she cried, reaching for him.

"Right here, Jen." He gave her his hand and let her squeeze until he could feel the bones bruising against one another. "Breathe! Don't push! Not yet. Too soon to push."

The contraction must have lasted almost a minute and a half, and when it was over she fell back, her face dewed with perspiration, dark circles beneath her eyes. She needed a cool cloth for her face and forehead, but he couldn't do everything. And what she wanted was certainly more important than what he wanted.

"Oh, God, that was the worst. I wanted to push so bad. When do I push?"

"I'll tell you, Jen, but not for a little while, not until I see the baby's crown, and then we have to wait until it wants to come on its own. Then you need to help, Jen, to push hard. The head can't come out too fast, though. That's bad, honey, but when the head begins to come on its own, then you push. I'll tell you."

"Jesus, you're a pro at this, aren't you?" she said.

"Just an experienced amateur. Help me now, because I need you sit up as much as you can." He took her own pillows and his, put one lengthwise below her back and shoulders, the others he placed sideways beneath her shoulders so she was half sitting. "Good. Are you comfortable?"

"You've got to be kidding?"

"Right. Stupid question. Are the pillows okay?"

"Sure, but another contraction is coming."

He quickly moved back and sat beside her, offering her his hand, which would really be sore tomorrow, a small reminder that she needed so much more than he could offer her. This time she thrashed her head from side to side and gritted her teeth.

"Hurts! Hurts so bad!"

"I know, sweetheart. I know. Hang in there. It will be over soon. Breathe, baby! Breathe! No pushing. Just breathe."

And again, she seemed to collapse when the the spasm had eased.

"Jenny, I need your cooperation."

"I thought I was cooperating," she said, licking her dry lips.

"I need Frau Holzman. Not for me, Jen, for you. Please."

"Can't we do it? Just you and me?"

"We will do it, Jen, just the two of us."

She looked at him pleadingly. "You won't let her take the baby, even for an instant! Promise, Erik. Nobody touches my baby but you. I'm so afraid . . . so afraid they'll take it from me . . . tell me I'm not fit."

"Oh, Jenny, Jenny, Jenny," he said, putting his cheek to her swollen flesh. "I'd never let that happen, and it never will. I swear to you. You are the most fit mother in the world."

"Okay then, if we really have to."

"I'd feel better, Jen."

"Okay."

"Frau Holzman!" he called, and hardly had the words left his mouth when she was there.

"Is everything all right?" she asked wide-eyed.

"Yes, but things are happening fast. I'd feel better if you were close. Jenny says it's okay. But nobody touches the baby except me. She's afraid that --"

"No reasons necessary. I do what I can."

"How about a cool washcloth, and maybe some ice for her to suck on . . . to eat."

"That I can do. Freda!" she called, and the young serving girl opened the door. They must have been camped right outside. "*Eis für die Dame.*"

"*Eis?*" she asked.

"*Ja, zerstossenes Eis zu essen.*"

"*Ach so!*" and she was gone.

Frau Holzman went to the bathroom and ran cold water over a washcloth, returned and cooled Jenny's forehead and face.

"Thank you, Frau Holzman. I've caused you so much trouble."

"*Nein*, my girl. You are the best of troubles."

"Ooooh, Erik, ooooh!" she cried.

"Don't push. Breathe -- blow, just don't push. I see the head, Jen! I see the head! Hold on."

He knew how hard it was for her, holding back, every muscle in her body wanting to help the baby out, but he had to make her wait. "Not yet, Jen. Breathe! Breathe! Breathe!" He could still see the dark head inside her spread opening. "Almost, honey, almost. Not quiet."

But as they waited, things seemed to be on hold. Every contraction would seem to push the small head closer, but then it would withdraw as the contraction eased, again and again, Jenny caught in a limbo of agony, and him incapable of easing her pain. "Breathe! Breathe! Breathe!" was all he could say.

And then as if by its own magic, the baby's head began to ease out of the birth canal. "Now, Jen, push, honey. Push. Push all you want . . . push all you can." And the enchantment held, the head slipping slowly between the folds of her stretched vagina, first the forehead, then the closed eyes, the tiny pug nose, finally the mouth and chin, the vagina finally closing a bit like a collar around the baby's small neck. "Head's out, Jen. Head's out." Without even thinking back to the instructions of the 911 operator, he carefully ran his thumb and forefinger down each side of the baby's nose to clear the

111

mucus and amniotic fluid, and then reaching down under the collar of Jenny's sex, he carefully did the same up the throat and under the chin, clearing out whatever fluids might have collected there. Another spasm took hold of her, and she cried out in pain.

"Push, Jen, push. You're doing great. Keep it up. I'm taking the baby's head now, and I'm going to push down very gently, very very gently, to help the front shoulder out. Now you have to push hard, honey . . . push hard for me . . . for your baby . . . we need the front shoulder, Jenny . . . push, sweetheart, push." As he urged her to push, she passed a hard, brown lump from her anus, and he reached quickly for a hand towel, cleaning her and removing the mess quickly with his right hand while holding the baby's head with his left. He gave the soiled cloth to Frau Holzman who took it to the bathroom, flushed it down the toiled and returned. "Push, Jenny!"

"I'm pushing as hard as I can, dammit!"

"I know you are, honey, and you're doing great. Just keep push -- it's coming, Jen, the shoulder's coming. I'm lifting the head so the rear shoulder can -- it's all sliding out, Jenny, your baby is almost here . . . almost . . . almost . . . here Jen. It's here!" It had come so quickly, and then he held it in his hands, bloody, slick and moving, held *her*, in his hands. "It's a girl, Jenny, a beautiful baby girl, just like you," he said, holding the baby up so Jenny could see, and in that instant the baby seemed to gulp air and began to cry.

"I want her, Erik. Give her to me." She stretched out her arms and tried to lift from her pillowed support.

"Just a second, honey, let me wrap her up. Towel," he said to Frau Holzman, and she held out a bath towel. He carefully wrapped the baby, and laid it on Jenny's stomach.

She took the baby and started to draw it up toward her.

"Careful, Jen, the cord hasn't been cut. Don't tug on it. Everything has gone perfectly so far, we don't want to tear something."

"She is beautiful, isn't she." She turned back the towel so she could see the baby's face while it lay on her stomach, a cap of fine, dark hair, even smeared with blood and her protective coating, she was beautiful.

"Like mother, like daughter," he said.

He and Frau Holzman watched mother and baby for a while, the baby's crying a satisfying tonic to both of them.

"Jenny, I either have to take her back now to cut the cord, or you have to hold her. Can you do that?"

"Will it hurt her?"

"I honestly don't know, but I have to do it."

"I don't want to give her up, Erik. I'll hold her."

"Frau Holzman, the shears and thread. I'll cut the cord, then you cut a good length of thread for me, okay."

"Yes, yes." She held the towel toward him and then opened it, offering the sharp kitchen shears.

He took them, held the cord several inches away from the baby's tummy, and cut through quickly. The baby's crying didn't seem any louder, and he hoped that it hadn't hurt her. He dropped the placenta end of the umbilical cord and folded the other back upon itself.

"Frau Holzman, the thread."

She handed him a length of the dark thread, and he wrapped it around the baby's cord several times tightly and then knotted it securely. "Now, Jenny, she's yours." He could feel the tension drain from his neck, shoulders and arms.

Jenny lifted the baby and held her against her naked breasts, and slowly she began to hush her crying until it settled into a series of small, regular gasps.

"You can hold her for a little, but I have to clean her. And the delivery isn't over, you know." His hand lay on her belly, now somewhat slack but still bloated, and he could feel another contraction rippling beneath his fingers, saw the grimace twist her smile.

When he had finally cleaned the cheesy coating, blood and amniotic fluid from the baby, Frau Holzman managed to find a small soft blanket in which he had wrapped the infant before giving her back to her mother. Some twenty minutes later the placenta had been expelled, and he had wrapped it in a towel. Strangely, Frau Holzman had taken it from him, and said that she had something special she would do with it.

"We did it," she said, rocking the baby back and forth in her arms, the sheet covering her once again.

"You did it, Jen. You were fantastic. Super."

"You were wonderful, Erik. I had no idea. You were so good, even when I yelled at you."

Frau Holzman suggested that Jenny would be a lot more comfortable if she could change the bedding, so they moved her to the other side, putting down several bath towels, while Frau Holzman changed the bloody sheets herself, brought in another rubber liner, and put everything, bloody liner, towels and sheets into a laundry bag.

When Frau Holzman had gone, Jenny said, "I feel like I'm still leaking down there."

"You are. But that's normal."

"I don't suppose I can take a shower. I feel all clammy and yucky, especially between my legs."

"I don't think so, Jen, but I'll help you wash up in bed, if vou'd like. I'll get you the basin and a wash cloth."

"Would you wash me, Erik?"

"If you want me to, of course."

Just as he got up, Frau Holzman was knocking at the door again. "I don't mean to disturb, Herr Leiden, but I thought these might help." She handed him a box of large sanitary pads. "From Freda's mother's last baby." Freda stood behind her, smiling nervously. She held a tray with a silver ice bucket, a bottle of German *Sekt*, and two glasses. Frau Holzman took the tray and handed it to him. "For you and Miss Jenny to make a toast, I think. From my husband and me. If you or she need anything before morning, please do call me. Yes?" She put a piece of paper down by the phone with her personal telephone number on it.

"Yes, you have been wonderful, Frau Holzman," he said, walking her to the door.

"Ach! You, sir, you are truly *ein Held*. I was so surprised."

"No hero. It all just kind of happened automatically."

"Not with the baby, with Miss Jenny. You were such a help. She loves you so, Herr Leiden, but I think she has had much sadness in her life. Take care of her. She is a good girl. Now, good night, and call if you have need."

"Thank you, and good night," he said as she left.

"Champagne?" Jenny asked as he walked back into the room.

"Yes, German champagne, it's called *Sekt*. The Holzman's have given it to us so we can make a toast."

"How nice."

"Do you want a bath or some bubbly first?"

"Both." She lifted her baby and kissed its tiny forehead.

He opened the bottle without popping the cork or gushing champagne, and poured them each a glass, fine bubbles wavering upward in bright, beaded chains. He handed her a glass.

"To Jenny Heilman, the bravest, most beautiful mother in the world, and her new baby," he said, lifting his glass.

"Couldn't she be *our* new baby, at least for tonight? We did all the hard part, didn't we? The easy part doesn't even matter any more."

He smiled at her, and held his glass a little higher. He had always dismissed the reality of a broken heart, had sided with

Shakespeare's dictum that men had died and worms had eaten them, but not for love; however, at that very moment, he felt as though his own were already cracking. He drank with her, having trouble getting the sparkling wine down his constricted throat.

"Now my turn. To you, Erik. You led me into the heart of a blizzard, and then gave me the sun. You don't have to love me, and I can't expect you to, but I want you to know how much I love you, and that I always will. I'll never take another breath without thanking whatever god or gods there are that they sat me next to you on that flight. Please don't say anything, just drink with me." She turned up her glass. "Now, do you still want to bathe me?"

"More than anything," knowing full well that to do so would be like thrusting his own hands into the flames of a roaring fire.

She separated the pillows and placed the baby between them on its back, and then he began to wash her narrow face and down her slender neck and throat, gently washing with soap and warm water, over her frail shoulders, setting her up and washing her back, her spine a lovely long line of raised baubles that he felt beneath the cloth, all the way down to her buttocks and between, rinsing, and squeezing the cloth to keep it fresh and clean, then back to her wonderfully full breasts, spending more time than necessary, probably, but unable to stop, even hazarding a kiss to one brown nipple.

"I love you so much," she whispered, but he only answered with a kiss to the other.

Then he washed down each slender arm, down to the hand, and separately each slim, graceful finger, before moving to her belly, still bloated, but no longer distended like it had been, on down between her legs.

"Nothing offends you, does it?"

"About you? How could it?"

"You even cleaned up my shit, didn't you? I barely remember it, but I know you did. Heard Frau Holzman flush it down the toilet." Huge tears rolled down her cheeks. "Jane Austen would have put you in a novel, I know."

"I'm afraid I would have been out of place in her world, Jen. I have trouble enough in my own."

As he washed her legs, she reached out a hand and ran her fingers down his cheek, across his lips. "You have the most wonderful face. It's like I can see your soul spread out across it, in your dancing green eyes, in your strong nose, in your generous and tender mouth. I see you, Erik . . . I know you . . . I love you." Her index finger ran down his nose, over his lips and down his chin.

When he had finished, he patted her dry, found her oversized tee shirt and helped her on with it. Several times between then and daylight he helped her go to the bathroom, stood beside her and held the baby while she urinated, and helped her change her pad.

Drapes open, the first reflected light, a golden rose that glowed from the powdery white landscape, seeped into the room. Farther south it was called the Alpenglow.

"Are you awake?" she asked him.

"Mmmm," he mumbled back.

"I know I've been a lot for you. Too much, I guess, but I want you to know I don't expect anything from you. You've already given me more than I could have dared to ask. I don't know exactly what it is, and I'm not asking you to tell me, but I know that you care about me, whether that's love or not, I don't know. I feel you come so close to me sometimes, almost as if we were sharing the same skin, sharing a single heart, and then something happens, and you pull away. I know there's lots to pull away from, Erik, but when you're close, that doesn't seem to matter to you. I just don't understand. I'm not smart about a lot of things, I just know that you're going to leave tomorrow. All I ask is that for the time we have left, if you feel like touching me, kissing me, holding me, you won't stop yourself. For one last day let me love you. Is that too much to ask?"

"Jen, you've asked nothing, but I have so little to give."

"You've given me my beautiful baby, you've given me the most wonderful Christmas I've ever had . . . you've given me a handful of happiness that outweighs all those years of feeling lost and alone. You've made me feel worth something, Erik, and now with my baby, I know what I have to do, the person I have to be. That's what you've given me. If you don't want to hold me and kiss me, I guess that's okay too. Just don't talk any more, okay?"

He moved to her, careful of the baby, found her face and held it between his hands, kissed her nose and eyes and lips, turned her face first left and then right, kissing each ear.

"You must know that I love you, Jen, have loved you from earlier on than even I understood, but it's more complicated than you know. I can't --"

She pulled him toward her with her left hand, holding the baby in her right, her kiss cutting him off in mid sentence. "Just please, please don't talk any more," she whispered against his lips, and then continued her kiss.

This time he didn't reason with himself, catalogue what-ifs and impossibilities. He returned her kiss as he had wanted to for so long.

"Yes, yes, yes," she spoke into his mouth, her lips open, her tongue seeking his, both knowing that there would be no sex, but driven by a stronger need, urged on by a desire for their tandem hearts to dance in unison in the rosehushed sunlight of that Christmas morning.

11

Sometime later he woke up. She was asleep in his arms, his left hand resting on the baby. He tried to extract his right arm from beneath her without waking her, but she stirred.

"No, don't get up. I feel so good when you hold me, so safe."

"I not leaving, Jen. I'm going to get us coffee and tea, and arrange for breakfast. What would you like?"

"All I want is more of your kissing. Do you know you have the softest lips?"

"There'll be more of that, but you have to eat, Jen. You have to drink. You've been through a lot. You have to worry about dehydration and replacing electrolytes and all that."

"You aren't drawing back, wiggling out of my grasp again, are you?" she asked, holding her baby with both arms, an exaggerated pout turning down her mouth.

"No, Jenny, no. I'm loving you right here and right now, in the only way I know how," he said seriously. "I'm trying to take care of you the best I can."

"Well, if you're sure. No herbal tea, then. I know I'm still supposed to watch what I eat and drink, for my milk when it comes in, but I want coffee this morning, lots of coffee, and lots of apple juice, and some of that *Bauernfrühstück*. It'll be kind of our last breakfast/lunch/supper, won't it? I don't have milk yet anyway."

He avoided the last, and said, "This is going to sound weird to you, but they usually don't make that at breakfast. I'll see what I can do, though. Anything you need for the baby? She'll need something to pass for diapers, won't she?"

"Yes, and powder and lotion, but that can wait a little, I guess. You've got me all excited," she said, sitting up in bed, smirking.

"Me or the breakfast?"

"Both!"

He returned some time later with a tray laden with two small silver coffee pots, another pitcher of hot milk, two large cups, and a large beer glass full of apple juice. Inside the door he stopped. She had her tee shirt pulled up and the baby nursed at one nipple. He stood watching them, Jenny's face just about as bright as the morning outside. He had never seen a sight more lovely.

"I have another one," she said, whether joking or serious he wasn't sure, but she lifted the full heavy breast toward him. "I want you so bad I could cry, Erik," and her eyes were moist with the wanting.

"I know the feeling, Jen, all too well. Another time, another place."

"But we're here and now, and there isn't going to be another time or another place, is there?"

"Love what we have right now, Jenny."

He stood a long time just watching her and the baby nursing. From time to time Jenny winced, but more often a half smile played upon her lips. "I know it's too soon for her to be getting any milk yet, but she sure is trying."

"Coffee?" he finally asked.

"Please."

Unexpectedly his own eyes filled with tears, and he turned away from her. "I don't even know . . . how . . . how you take your coffee," he said with a catch in his throat.

"I want it just the way you have it. I want to taste what you taste. I want to feel what you feel. I would give anything to know what you know. I want to be as gentle and as kind and as caring as you are. I want that for my baby, Erik, I want to be a mother like you must have been a father."

"Careful, Jen. I've got lots of flaws. I don't think a boy becomes a drug addict all on his own, and my wife, well, you know about that. And if you hadn't fallen into my life, I would be spending Christmas alone, instead of with my own Madonna and Child. Don't make me something I'm not, Jenny. I'm just a man. Just a man."

"I'm not a school girl, Erik. I don't have a crush on you. I know what you are, sometimes I think maybe better than you do. Sure, you're just a man, but you are the best man I have ever known. And once again, you're talking too much. No hedges today, Erik, no fences, or walls or barriers. Try to just be with me this last day."

He didn't answer, rather he poured her coffee into the Rosenthal cup up to a little over half, then hot milk the rest of the way, followed by two heaping spoons of sugar. He stirred it and then carried it to her. She took the cup and he held the saucer as she drank.

"Mmmmm. Just like I had hoped, hot, rich and sweet. Can you set the saucer here on the nightstand? I want you to get yours and come sit by me. If I can help it, I'm not going to let you out of my sight today."

He poured his own coffee and brought her apple juice and placed it beside her saucer. "Oh, by the way, someone will be bringing you a plate of *Baurenfrühstück* shortly."

"Oh, wonderful, or is it *wunderbar?*"

"You stay here another week and you'll be fluent."

"The only thing I want to be fluent in is you. I wish I could stay here forever -- we could stay here for ever."

He turned his head away, but she took his chin and turned it back. "I'm sorry. That wasn't fair. I'm just so happy. I know there's a flip side to all of this for you that I don't seem to understand, but I'll try not to do that again. Promise. I'll really try hard. I can't help being happy, but I don't want to make you unhappy. I never want you to be unhappy."

In a short while Frau Holzman herself brought the tray, a large one with a huge serving dish of the farmer's breakfast, two plates, and two red roses. Where had she managed to find them in this weather, the roads impassible, cut off from the rest of the world? Behind her came Freda carrying a large wicker basket lined with small pillows and a blanket, on the handle a pink ribbon tied in a large bow.

"For the baby, if you want," she said.

"How nice, Frau Holzman. You have been so understanding. I can't ever thank you enough for all you have done. And I've been so much trouble for you and everyone else."

"Nice troubles, as I have said before. Very nice troubles. And where would you want this?"

"Here, let me take it," he said, and put the tray on the table in the sitting room.

"She is a beautiful baby, Miss Jenny. Not all . . . all . . . how do you say *schrumplig*?" she asked him, but he shook his head. "*Wie die Backpflaume*," she added.

"Oh, like a prune. You're right, she isn't all wrinkly like a prune, Frau Holzman," he agreed.

Jenny lifted the infant and kissed her gently, turned her toward the older woman. "Yes, she is beautiful, isn't she." The wet little mouth worked as if searching for her mother's nipple.

"*So, guten Appetit!* And you must rest today. You worked so hard last night. The doctor comes between ten and eleven, I think."

"Thank you again for everything, Frau Holzman," Jenny said as the woman left.

"Frau Holzman told me the strangest thing this morning," he said. "I don't know if you remember, but she took away the placenta in a towel, and said she was going to do something special with it. Well, she had her husband dig down through the snow by the big fir tree in front, use a pick-ax to break up the frozen ground and bury the placenta. It's supposed to bring good luck to the baby and to you. She says it goes back to the days when the Germanic tribes were still worshiping trees. Isn't that strange?"

"Strange or not, I like it. Who would believe they would go to so much trouble for me and my baby? I think it's all because of you."

"Nonsense, Frau Holzman dotes on you. So, do you want breakfast in bed, or do you want to try and get up?"

"I really think I'd like to try and sit at the table, if I can."

"Okay, let's give it a try." He went and got the wicker basket and sat it at the foot of the bed. "Let me take the baby."

She handed her daughter to him without hesitation. The baby whimpered, but never broke into crying. Jenny watched him gently put her inside. "What better baby carrier could you have? It's perfect," he said.

Then he moved to her and helped her swing her legs over the edge of the bed. She grimaced, and clutched his upper arm.

"Okay?"

"Just sore. I wish it was because we had made love all night, but --" As he began to help her stand, she sat back down. "Oooh, I've bled through the pad." She lifted the tail of her tee shirt. It too was bloody.

"No problem. You stay there, and we'll get you cleaned up. Arms up. Let's get your tee shirt off." He was careful to keep the dark, damp stain away from her skin. "Now this," he said, unfastening the pad in front from the elastic belt. "Lean forward." She did and he freed the pad in back. "Lie down, and I'll be right back."

"I'm all sticky," she said, lying there with her legs spread.

123

"We'll fix that." He sat the basin of warm soapy water on the bed, and took the washcloth, wrung it slightly, and began to wash the blood and discharge from between her legs.

"You are amazing, Erik Leiden. Nothing offends you. I'm a bloody, smelly mess, and you just go on like it was nothing. You clean up my shit and where it came from without a hint of disgust."

"Nothing about you could ever disgust me, Jen, nothing." He rolled her slightly and washed between her cheeks, around her anus, high up her crack, rinsed the cloth, and did it all again. By now the water in the basin was dark. "Be still, and I'll get fresh water, and then you'll be as good as new."

When he had finished, he toweled her dry, patted softly around her vagina, and finally bent and kissed her low on the belly. She grabbed his head and held his face against her now slack stomach for one fierce moment before she released him.

"Now, do you have another tee shirt?"

"I'm afraid not. I could wear one of my dresses, I suppose."

"I've a better idea." He went to the free standing closet and took one of his shirts off its hanger, felt it, rubbed it against his cheek, and walked back to her. "Try this. It's pretty soft, 100% cotton." He handed her the shirt.

"It's fine. The nicest part is that it's yours. I hope you don't want it back." She clutched the shirt to her full, naked breasts. He just smiled at her.

She put on the shirt, buttoned it up the front, telling him they were on the wrong side, and finally rolled up the sleeves to her elbows. When she finished, he stood there holding out a new pad.

"No, you." And he deftly connected the pad to its belt, all the while being gently attacked by her kisses anywhere she could find bare flesh.

He carried the baby's basket on one arm and helped her with the other. Setting the basket on the table, he told her to stand holding the chair for an instant, and he hurried back to the bed and got a pillow for her to sit on. Then they devoured the heaping platter of *Bauernfrühstück*, she spearing the last few morsels of cubed potato and ham that still clung to the platter with her fork.

"What are you smiling at?"

"I love to watch you eat. It's nice to see a woman who really enjoys food."

"See what you will be mis -- sorry!" She clamped her teeth and lips tightly together.

The phone's ringing saved the moment, though. He walked to the night stand and picked it up, nodded his head a lot, and then hung it up. "The doctor is on his way up, and they are clearing the road, so I have to go down to the car. Do you want me to stay while the doctor is here?"

"Yes, of course, but no. You go on. I know you have to get your ox out of the ditch, or whatever it is."

In just a few minutes the doctor and Frau Holzman arrived, him carrying his black bag, and Frau Holzman carrying several large containers of disposable diapers. The doctor was young and blond, a little too young for Erik's liking, but he did have to go and see about the car. Frau Holzman introduced everyone around, and the Herr Doktor Fleischer looked back and forth quickly between Miss Heilman and Mr. Leiden. Erik smiled to himself, pulled on his coat and gloves, kissed her, and told her that he would be back just as soon as he could.

Almost an hour later he returned to find Jenny sitting up in bed, still wearing his shirt, but opened down the front, nursing the baby, her other breast half covered. "Is everything okay? The baby? You?" He asked, a bit alarmed because her eyes look red and a bit puffy.

"Yes, we did an excellent job." She gave a faint smile. "Erika is in perfect health."

"Erika?"

"Yes, Erika. The doctor had to fill out a form of some kind, maybe a birth certificate, I don't know, and I had to come up with a name. I hope you don't mind."

"Mind? I'm thrilled, Jenny, and touched beyond words. Erika, little Erika . . . but you, how are you?"

"I'm fine too. You did everything right, my love. Everything. When I told him, the doctor was amazed. See, you are amazing. We are both in perfect health, and in a few days, we can go home."

"That's wonderful, Jen. Wonderful." But the look on her face didn't seem the least bit happy.

"And how is your ox?"

"Ox? Oh, the car. Well, they plowed the road, on Christmas Day, can you imagine, and a farmer with a tractor pulled the car out of the snow bank. It's not much the worse for wear, really. Kind of buckled the door panels is about all. Anyway, the insurance will cover it." He stood looking at her and the baby. "Can I hold her?"

"Of course, you can." She separated the sucking mouth from her nipple, and the baby whimpered just a little as she held the pink bundle up to him.

"I think she looks like you, Jen. I really do. She's lucky."

"I hope she is luckier than I've been, Erik. I look like me, and that hasn't helped a whole lot."

"No, but she has *you* for a mother, and that will make all the difference." He walked around the room, up into the sitting room, and back, humming to the baby girl, unaware of the tears that collected in her mother's lavender eyes.

He encouraged her to have a light lunch, because he had planned a special dinner, making sure again that she didn't want to watch her diet. "I want to eat anything you feed me,

Erik. Today I have special . . . what's that word . . . it means permission, but I've forgotten."

"Dispensation," he helped.

"Yes, dispensation. Today I have special dispensation. One last day of gluttony before you leave. Erika says she will allow it, just this once."

He just smiled and shook his head. And the afternoon they spent lying on the bed, holding hands, touching, kissing occasionally, the baby always between them, mostly just being together, but late in the afternoon she looked at him seriously, those lavender eyes quizzical. "Can I ask you something I have no right to ask?" She reached out and touched his hand, one finger running up and down the back.

"Sure, Jen, whatever," he said with a long sigh.

"I just want to know how your wife could have divorced you. I know it's none of my business -- I have no right at all, but . . . well . . . it just doesn't make any sense to me. You are so --"

"*Me*, Jen, I'm so *me*, and she just got tired of me. I won't go into all the details, but I'll tell you what she told me. She said that the passion had gone out of our marriage. 'The fire is gone,' I believe that's how she put it. That was about a year after she had had a hysterectomy. She just became a different woman, not that she was ever easy. But I guess she tried to find that passion someplace else, with someone else. She had always been self-centered, hot-tempered, but also vivacious. In many ways she was everything I wasn't, and that's probably what attracted me in the first place. She had been to all the places I hadn't, schools in France and Switzerland, had seen all the things I probably never would. We lived in two different worlds most of the time. I was always early; she was always late. But when you live with someone that long, even the flaws and irritations become a part of the structure that supports your life. When she left, all that crumbled. I'm one of those old-fashioned types, 'till death do us part' and all. I would have stuck it out to the end, no matter how bad it had gotten, I suppose.

"Then the divorce was messy. I made a lot of money, but we had a lot of debt -- the more I made, the more she spent -- no, that's not fair, really, the more *we* spent. I had to sell off so much to pay off all that debt, and she walked away pretty much unscathed. California isn't a very friendly state for such things. She lives in Switzerland with a psychiatrist. So, there you have it. Erik Leiden, a man without passion."

"You and I both know that isn't true. Thank you though, I just wondered how someone could walk away from you. I could never leave you, Erik." She lifted, bent and kissed the hand that she had stroked all through the telling.

Ah, but he could leave her, couldn't he? Would, as a matter of fact, the very next day. He only wished that there were some way to spare her the hurt he knew would come with his departure, but he saw no way of doing that.

"Dinner is at seven, you said?"

She had saved him from having to respond to her confession. "Yes, around that. Frau Holzman will call us when they are ready to send it up. Why?"

"You said that I could probably take a shower tonight. I feel yucky, and I know I smell."

"Did you ask the doctor?"

"No, I don't need the doctor. I have you. Is it okay?"

"If you feel strong enough, I suppose."

"If you'll help me, I'd like to try it."

"Okay, let's do it." He got up and went around the bed.

"Don't leave the baby here, though. I want her with us."

"Of course, but lets get you ready first." He unbuttoned the shirt, and took it off one sleeve at a time, noticing that the breast that the baby had nursed from was somewhat raw and irritated, displaying small drops of clear liquid. Soon she

128

would have real milk. "Off with the belt and pad." She managed herself, and he took the blood stained padding and put it in the bathroom. Returning, he was caught in mid-stride by her loveliness, from her short bobbed hair, along her elegant neck, the slim width of her shoulders, and those full, full breasts, all of her naked before him, even if her belly was still puffy and slack.

"Now you," she said, startling him.

"Me?"

"Yes, you. I want you to shower with me -- unless you don't want to."

"Of course I want to, but do you think that's a good idea?"

"Yes, a very good idea. I want to see you without your clothes. You've seen probably every inch of me, but I've seen very little of you. Think of it as a mental snapshot that I'll get to keep. I know, I know, I'm getting close to the line again, but I want this, Erik. Is it so much to ask? Unless you really don't want to."

"If that's what you want, that's what I want, Jen." Turning slightly away from her, he unbuttoned his shirt, took it off slowly and threw it across the foot of the bed, unbuckled his belt, unclasped his pants, unzipped them, and finally pulled them down over his narrow hips and stepped out of them one leg at a time. He stood before her in his jockey shorts, aware that he was half hard.

"Go on, you're doing fine. Breathe! Breathe!"

"Not funny, Jen. This is difficult for me. I don't think you know what you are asking."

"Yes I do, and it's not what I'd really like to ask, so just humor me, okay?"

He slipped his thumbs inside the waist band and shucked them off. "There, satisfied?"

"No, turn and look at me. I want to look at you."

He slowly turned and faced her. "Now?"

"Very. You're beautiful, all of you. I know you think you're old, too old for me and all, but you're not. You're perfect for me. I wish you could see that."

He didn't even try to reason with her. She would simply tell him again that he was talking too much.

Then her mouth fell open and her hand move up to cover it. "What is that . . . what happened?" She went to him, reached out and touched the large starburst of silky white scar tissue that spread beneath his right collarbone and all the way to his shoulder joint.

"Old wound, Jen. Old wound."

She gently ran her fingers over the scar, tiptoed and kissed it across its jagged width and height. "Tell me."

"It's one of those things *I* try not to think about, Jen."

"Did you get that in the Gulf War?"

"Aaaah, Jenny," he said, shaking his head with a pained smile, even more painfully aware of the real gulf that separated them. "Vietnam, Jen, the dark ages for you, but the scar's nothing. The least painful part of it all. I was a Lieutenant, 101st Airborne . . . I lost a whole squad of men, Jen . . . every last one of them. We were surprised in the Tet Offensive, and I lost every one of those young men who trusted me, relied on me to get them through that living hell. But I failed them, Jen . . . couldn't even get myself out. I used to have nightmares too, Jenny, horrible nightmares, all those boys, slaughtered, butchered by mortar and machine gun fire, crying out for me to help them, and there was absolutely nothing I could do. And they gave me the Bronze Star, almost an insult -- for surviving, I suppose." He shook his head and said, "This is the real star, Jen, the hard reminder of just who I am," and he touched the scar with his own finger tips.

"It couldn't have been your fault, Erik. How could it?" She put her cheek against his chest.

"I was their commander, Jen. They trusted me." He looked away from her, but she turned his face back toward her own, his green eyes bright with pain.

"I love you beyond words, Erik Leiden," and then she put her arms beneath his and around his chest, held him silently, held him until the trembling stopped. Neither spoke for a long while, and then she finally said, "Get Erika, and let's take a shower."

The hot water felt good, and they left the door open so that the bathroom wouldn't get too steamy for the baby. It was certainly steamy in the shower, though. He soaped the cloth and washed her from head to toe, her face and neck, across her shoulders and back, around and between her high, heavy breasts, "Careful," she had cautioned because her nipples were so tender, and then down her belly.

"God, how I wish I weren't so sore there," she said as he knelt and ran the cloth up between her legs, up the crack of her buttocks. She took his wrist and stopped his hand on her sex. "Just hold it there. Press, but not too hard. That's it. If you can't love me, I can accept that, but just tell me that you know how much I love you."

"I think I know, Jen. That's what hurts so bad. I really think I know."

He washed down each leg, and lifted each foot, her balancing with a hand on his shoulder and the other against the tiled wall, washed between her toes, and finally bent and kissed each one when he had finished.

"Now me you," she said, taking the cloth from him.

"I'm not so sure you should do that."

"I'll just do what I can. I promise."

"Okay, but be careful."

"You hold me." And he did, while she soaped the cloth, washed his face, and neck and throat, his chest, gently over the scar, kissing it once, getting soap on her lips and mouth, but he

131

would not let go of her so she could do his back. Instead, she put her arms under his, her breasts moving against his chest, nipples hard, and soaped his back as best she could.

He could feel himself growing erect as her slick breasts and hard nipples rubbed against him, as her belly and thighs brushed against his own. "I'm sorry, Jen, I can't help it."

"I know, I know," she said, and reached for him, moved her hand up and down.

He turned away from her. "Don't, Jenny. Oh, God, don't. I don't think I could stand it. God how I want you, Jen . . . but not like that . . . and not just once . . . not for just one night . . that would be unbearable."

He pulled her face up toward his, kissed her fiercely, afraid that his need might suck the very soul up out of her breast. "Jen . . . Jen . . . Jen . . ." he mouthed against her eager lips, drawing her as close as he could without crushing her, forgetting the hardness that throbbed between them, trying desperately to forge a unity that he knew could never be. He was glad that the shower's spray hid his tears.

12

Frau Holzman's call came just as they had finished dressing, her back in his shirt, saying she would probably never take it off again.

Johann and Freda accompanied her, both carrying large trays with covered plates and dishes, a large soup tureen, and she managing two tray stands, a wine bucket and a bottle of wine in a green bottle.

Under one arm Frau Holzman carried a linen cloth, which she spread on the table. Freda had two candles tucked under her free arm, and Johann silver candle sticks beneath his. In seconds the table had been laid, the candles lit, the wine opened, and the soup ladled up.

"*Guten Appetit,*" they all said as they marched out, Freda and Johann looking at them and each other as though they had some special bond between them.

"No toasts tonight, Jen. Let's just enjoy the wine."

She held the glass up to the light and looked at its pale gold body. "I know it's not a very sophisticated thing to say, but it's pretty."

"Yes it is, and it tastes even better."

She put the glass to her lips and sipped. "Mmmmmmmm. It's wonderful. I haven't had much wine, but this is like drinking . . . I don't know what. Ambrosia? No, that's the food, isn't it. What's the word I want?"

"Nectar."

"Yes, it's like drinking nectar. No wonder they were always drunk and screwing around." She took another drink. "Is this a story wine?"

"What do you mean?"

"Have you been where it's grown? Do you know the owner? Did you drink too much in his cellar and have to spend the night? You know, a wine with a story."

"Yes, I suppose so, but that's not why I ordered it. I just thought you'd like it. I do."

"See?"

"See what?"

"Nothing." She shook her head, smiling slightly.

"Well, you do like it, don't you?"

"What do you think?" She took another drink. "Go on, a quick story, the soup smells too good to wait."

"Quick story. It's a 1994 Trittenheimer Altärchen Spätelese. Know the owner. Godfather of his daughter. Got too busy making money, and lost touch. Miss him. And it is one of my favorite wines. Short enough."

"God, but I love you. Now the soup. What is it?"

"Not native to the Bavarian Forest. Borrowed from the Allgäu, in the south-west of the state of Bavaria. It's called *Allgäuer Käsesuppe*, cheese soup. Butter, one beaten egg, flour, beef stock, milk, thick cream, Emmentaler, salt, pepper, a hint of nutmeg. On top, croutons and crumbled bacon. Don't know the cheese maker, never met his wife. That's all, folks."

"You're crazy."

"That may be, but I have good taste in mothers."

"See." She made a face and spooned up some of the cheese soup. "Wow! Now that's an 'oh-my-god' if I ever tasted one. Cheese soup? You were serious?"

"Dead serious."

"I hope there's lots left."

"More than you will be able to eat -- what's more, I want you to save room for the rest of dinner and dessert."

"Yes, daddy -- oh, shit! Shit! Shit!" She bit the corner of her bottom lip and tears collected quickly in her eyes. "Forgive me, I was just trying to be funny," she said, her pretty face twisted into a painful grimace.

"I know, Jenny, the other stuff just keeps creeping in, doesn't it?"

"Please forget I said that. That was so stupid. It's not like that for me, Erik, it really isn't. I just -- I'm so sorry. Just please forget I said it, please." She moved her spoon back and forth across the bottom of her empty soup plate.

"It's okay, Jen, don't worry about it."

"No more soup for me, I guess?" she finally said, trying to smile through her tears.

"Just a little, if you really like it that much." He took her bowl and ladled another small helping into it, which she finished slowly, head down, looking up at him from time to time, lavender eyes still bright with tears. Finally she took a deep breath and said, "Now what?"

"Upscale peasant food." He removed their soup bowls, and replaced them with dinner plates on which three finger length sausages rested on a bed of something stringy with half a dozen golden pretzel-like objects fanned around the top of the plate.

"Sausages?"

"Yes, *Nürnbergerwürstchen* over a creamed sauerkraut, surrounded by potato pretzels. Not really pretzels, they're just made in the shape of pretzels."

She cut into one of the *wurst* and took a bite. "It's very good." And then she took a small forkful of sauerkraut, smelled it, looked at him and then put the fork into her mouth. "Mmmm," and she went back for more, smiling. "Sauerkraut? No!"

He nodded, and enjoyed his own. Next they had a rich *Veal Ragout Fin* in a light, flaky pastry shell, followed by *Kaiserschmarren mit Apfelmus.*

"What an interesting dessert," she said, finishing up what had looked like a thick pancake that had been torn apart and spread with the most delicious apple sauce.

"That wasn't dessert. It's just a local dish that I thought you'd like. Dessert is yet to come. I have to call Frau Holzman for that, though," and he got up and made the call.

"There's just a little wine left. Would you like it?"

"You wouldn't try to get a girl drunk, would you?"

"Only if she wanted me to, but you should know that there is another bottle of wine coming."

"I sure hope you don't want me to pass out."

"Not a chance. We'll make it last. It's not like what we've been drinking anyway."

The knock at the door announced Frau Holzman, with a smaller tray on which she carried two silver bowls, one filled with something that looked like white pudding, the other chocolate, and another smaller green bottle stood on the tray as well.

"Has everything tasted good?" she asked him, setting the bottle of wine on the table, moving all the dishes and plates onto one tray so she could set down the one she held.

"You will have to ask Jenny, Frau Holzman."

"Was everything to your liking?"

"Everything was wonderful -- *wunderbar*. And what do we have in those silver bowls?"

"*Bayerische Creme, Weisse und Schokolade*. Bavarian cream, vanilla and chocolate."

"Mm, sounds yummy."

"Thank you." Seemingly effortlessly, she lifted the tray with all the dishes, hooked the stand with her free arm and opened the door. "When you wish, just call, and I will clear away things."

Instead of opening the wine, Frau Holzman had left a corkscrew on the table. "Wine with dessert or after?" he asked her.

"I don't know. You tell me."

"Why don't we wait, then."

He took her dessert plate and with a large silver spoon carefully curled up a large roll of the white dessert, which he placed gently off center on her plate. Then he did the same with the chocolate.

"You are a multi-talented person, aren't you?" She was looking at him, but there was no hint of a smile. "I could never have done that. You say you have no interest in cooking, but I'll bet you're a closet chef."

"I make a pretty good sandwich, but that's about as complicated as it gets. But I want you to know that I'm a truly gifted eater," he said, smiling at her as he scooped up another spoonful of cream, less carefully than before, and put it on his own plate.

They both took a spoonful of the dessert, and the same raptured look crossed their faces.

"Heavenly," she said, eyes closed, letting the dessert dissolve on her tongue.

"It is sensational, isn't it?"

"Now this I'm having seconds of, even if I have a belly-ache in the night. Speaking of closets, did I tell you that I live in one?"

"A closet?"

"Yeah, a real closet. Well, it used to be a walk-in closet in this big old house in Hollywood. But now it's my bedroom -- my cell. I have this narrow little bed, and use the clothes rack that was already there. I have a little night stand, and a chair and a small table. And books, now."

"You really live in a closet?"

"I'm serious. I don't mind though. It's cheap, and I have my privacy. I'm like a nun, I guess -- a nun with a baby now, how's that?"

Yes, he wondered just how that would be, but he didn't want to think about it, so he said, "With books, too, though. What kind of books?"

"Oh, gee, all kinds. You know I told you I'm really stupid -- no, ignorant. I have to remind myself of that. So when I found out I was pregnant, I decided I had to do something about that, 'cause I didn't want my baby to have an ignorant mother. So I started reading. I'd find these booklists, you know, things everybody should have read and all. I couldn't afford to buy books, so I used the library a lot."

"You are something else, Jenny."

"I told you that my baby is going to have it better than I did, Erik. I'll do everything I can to make sure of that."

"I have no doubt of it, Jen. None whatsoever. So who do you like to read?"

"You'll laugh."

"When have I laughed at you?"

"Never."

"Okay, who are you reading right now?"

"I have a paperback of *Persuasion* in my duffel bag, but I haven't been doing any reading, thanks to you."

"Jane Austen?"

"Yes, I love her. I love her characters and stories -- and her happy endings, I guess. I know the world isn't that way, but I think maybe it should be."

Their conversation had been punctuated by bites of Bavarian cream, and she had even finished her first helping and was well into a second without even knowing it, but when she discovered he had given her more, she said, "Hey, isn't there a law against contributing to the gluttony of a new mother?"

"I hope not."

They ate silently, even sat quietly after they had finished, her reaching for his hand across the table, but saying nothing. She ran her finger across the hills and valleys of his knuckles, stroked slowly back and forth, again and again.

"That was the best meal I have ever had," she said, breaking the long silence. "Even better than the Christmas feast. Our last supper was the best, Erik. I've had a lifetime of bests in these few short days, thanks to you." She gave his hand a hard squeeze and then let it go with a deep, shuddering sigh.

"Wine?"

"I don't really think I have any room."

"I'll pour you just a little then, but you have to at least taste it."

"A story wine?"

"Everything has a story, but I'll spare you. I just want you to taste this."

With the same deftness with which he had served the Bavarian Creme, he opened the knife end of the corkscrew, ran it around the capsule topping the bottle's neck, snapped it shut, and then drew out the screw, inserting it into the top of the cork, and after several quick twists, bent the handle down and place the notched brace on the lip of the opening. With a steady lift the cork came out with a slight pop.

She shook her head. "You are so graceful at everything you do."

"No, I've just opened a few bottles of wine in my day, Jen."

The two glasses that he poured the wine into were smaller than the ones they had used for the wine with dinner.

"This is special stuff, isn't it."

"Very. Just for you."

"How special?" The wine that flowed into her glass was a dark amber, and just as soon as it began to splash into the small bowl of the glass, she could smell it.

"It's an *Eiswein*, Jen. Maybe once in a decade they even get to make this stuff. It's always a gamble. They have to leave the grapes on the vines until late. When a freeze comes, they have to pick the grapes while they are still frozen. Nasty work, if you want to know the truth. Anyway, the grapes have to be crushed when they are frozen."

"Water freezes," she said, "so what they get is like pure grape juice, like the essence of the grape," she said, smiling.

"Exactly, Jen, and don't ever think you're stupid, you understand me? You are as bright as they come. Pure grape juice is what they get, loaded with residual sugar. The wine from those grapes, and this is an Ockfener Bockstein, 1976, is kind of like a rare and precious oddity. This particular wine was exceptional, but it has had a long life, like me, and I hope it's still good. Herr Holzman says that he has taken great care with the half dozen bottles he had. Let's try it, and see if it lives up to its reputation."

"*Eiswein*, right?" she asked. "Ice and wine?"

"Yes, exactly."

She lifted it to her lips and then stopped. "I'll bet it's expensive."

"Just think of it as drinking gold."

"If some other man were telling me this, he would just be trying to impress me, get me into bed or something, but I know you're not."

"I think the last time I tried to impress you was on the plane, some stupid comment about trying the Wehlener Sonnenuhr."

"Why are you doing this then?"

"It's about all I have to give you, Jen. It's who I am and what I do. The money isn't important. The only important thing is that you get to taste some of me."

"That I understand. Thank you for such a precious piece of yourself." She put the glass to her lips and took a small swallow. The smile was involuntary, her mouth opening. "Oh,

Erik. It's better than gold. You were right, I'm drinking *you*. This is exactly what you taste like, isn't it?" She took another drink. "See what can come out of the cold? Out of the ice and snow?"

He drank from his own, the thick, sweet liquid warming him, her words seductive, but he knew that making lives was even harder than making wine. "Let me call and have them clear the table, and we can finish our wine in more comfort."

And they did. By the time they had finished the bottle, he felt lightheaded, unusual for him. It was eleven, and he had to get up early if he was going to make his flight.

"Are we gong to leave her in the basket, or are we going to take her to bed?" he asked her.

"I don't want anything between us tonight. Would you bring one of the chairs over from the table. If I set her right next to me on the chair, she'll be all right, won't she?"

"I'm sure she will."

He brought the chair, and they positioned the baby's basket. Then Jenny pulled off her shirt and looked at him as he began to undress. "One last favor?"

"Sure, Jen, if I can."

"Don't wear your pajamas tonight. I know we're not going to make love -- can't, and you wouldn't if we could. But for tonight, I want to sleep with your body against mine. I want to feel you next to me. Nothing in between."

He nodded his head, agreeing against his better judgment. "But I'm not Gandhi, Jenny."

"I never asked you to be Gandhi. I'm quite content with you being you, but if it's going to be torture or something, never mind." She reached for her shirt.

"It's not torture in the sense you mean, Jen. If I were somebody else, but I'm not." Even as he spoke, he was stripping off his shirt and trousers, taking off his shoes and socks, and finally his shorts.

141

"I love looking at you. I could look at you forever."

"I know the feeling, Jenny. Too well."

"Come," she said, and moved so that he would have room on her half of the bed. "Just hold me, Erik. You don't have to do anything beyond that. I just want to feel your skin against mine."

He took her in his arms, and she nestled against him until she found comfortable bends and hollows, and then settled in. And when he spoke her name, she said, "No talking, dearest. Not a word." And she found ways to get even closer to him, easing farther into an soft indentation here, a muscled nook there.

In the night he woke to the baby's whimpering. He waited a second, but Jenny slept on. He knew that she had to be exhausted, so he got up and picked up the infant, held her and opened the blanket so he could feel the tiny diaper. It seemed damp, but he didn't know if it was damp enough to change. He carried her into the bathroom, closed the door and turned on the light, and the baby cried harder in the sudden brightness.

"Shssh, my pet, shsssssssh, Daddy's gonna make it all better." He put a towel down on the counter and laid her upon it. "'Hush little baby, don't say a word' . . ." he sang to her, and her crying slowly eased . . . "'Daddy's gonna buy you a mocking bird' . . ." dwindled to a whimper. With the same deftness with which he did most things, he had her changed in seconds. He wrapped her back up and turned off the light, and with the light off, she did little more than utter tiny gasps and gurgles, but once back in the bedroom, he didn't return her to her basket. He knew that he would probably never hold her like this again. "'And if that mocking bird don't sing, Daddy's gonna buy you a diamond ring,'" he sang softly, hoping not to wake Jenny. He knew it didn't make any sense, but he felt like the baby was partly his, as much his as that of the blank face that had fathered her. Hadn't he as well as Jenny brought her into the world? "'And if that diamond rings turns brass . . .'" Hadn't they done it together, as a team?

He continued to walk back and forth across the room at the foot of the bed, just as he had his own tiny daughter all those years ago. "'Daddy's gonna buy you a looking glass...'" He had been the one who had gotten up in the dead of night and given her that one-thirty feeding, and then up again only a few hours later to go to work. And when she was older, he had been the one to hear her crying in the night, the one who had comforted her when a bad dream had frightened her awake. Those same feelings worked in him now as he paced back and forth, singing softly, turning his shoulders back and forth, rocking her, rocking her, loving her there in his arms for perhaps the last time.

Finally, he could hear the small, steady whisper of her breathing, and thought he should put her down before she woke again. As he did, he became aware that Jenny was awake, raised on one elbow, looking at him.

"What are you doing up?" he whispered.

"Watching you . . . listening to you . . . loving you . . . but most of all, missing you, and you aren't even gone yet."

He climbed back into bed beside her, and she moved to him quickly. "Jen, I --"

Her kiss stifled his words.

"No talking, remember," she said and kissed him again.

They fell asleep kissing, and then sometime before daylight, he woke to find her clutching him, his chest wet with her tears. She was still wrapped in his arms, so he didn't move. What could he hope to do that would comfort her? He himself was the source of her misery, and making her even more aware of him wouldn't help her in the least. Telling her that he was

143

leaving for her own good wouldn't salve the ache either. He wasn't even sure if it was true.

As much as he loved her, wanted her, did he possibly want something else even more? Simplicity? A life without complication? Was it the difficulties that were driving him away? The difference in age? The baby? The reaction of his family? Jenny was younger than his own daughter. Oh, the complications, the complexities, the entanglements that would come, and come they surely would. Was he saving her from them? Was he sparing her a trek through the Hyrcanian wood, or himself? All he could do was cling to her as he rode out the night, weathered the onslaught of unanswered questions.

The alarm in his head told him that it was close to six o'clock and he had to get up. His first thought was not to wake her, but he remembered their first morning together. "Jen, honey, I have to get up."

She came to life slowly, but knowingly. "Noooo, stay. A little longer. Just a little."

"I can't, Jen. I have to pack and take care of things here and still catch that plane. You stay in bed, and I'll be as quiet as I can."

She held his hand, but he pulled away, and her's fell back on the bed. She managed to raise and prop herself on one elbow, her chin and jaw on her hand. He turned on the bathroom light and closed the door so that just a crack fell into the room, and in that wedge of brightness she watched him dress, covering the long supple body that had lain warm and naked beside her own during the night. She watched him pack, swiftly and efficiently.

"I'm going downstairs to settle up. Can I bring you coffee?"

"No. I may give up coffee. I'm in a giving up mood, it seems."

"Don't make it any harder than it is, Jenny."

"I'm not, Erik. The hurt is doing just fine on its own. It doesn't need any help. You've given me my greatest joy, and now, through no fault of your own, my greatest pain."

"I didn't mean it to be like this."

"I know you didn't, Erik. Watching you with the baby last night nearly broke my heart. You were so good, so gentle, so loving. And she's not even yours. Just like when you helped me on the plane. You can't help being who you are, and I love you for it, and I'm sure you think you're doing the right thing, but it just isn't the right thing for me."

He didn't bother to try and explain his feelings. "I have to go down, but I'll be back up before I leave."

He closed the door behind him quietly.

Downstairs Frau Holzman was behind the desk, checking out an older couple. She looked up at him in surprise, but went about her business. He took the opportunity to get a cup of coffee from the breakfast room while she finished up.

"You are leaving after all?"

"I must, Frau Holzman. I have a business appointment tomorrow in Los Angeles. I have to be there. I don't have any choice. It's better like this anyway."

She gave him a stern look. "For you? Miss Jenny? And what of them, Miss Jenny and the baby?"

"That's what I want to talk with you about. I want to pay for the room and meals that we have had, but I want to leave the credit card account open if possible. I want Jenny and the baby to stay as long as she wants. I will sign the slip now. You just bill my account for whatever the final charge is. Can you do that?"

"But of course, Herr Leiden," she said, casting a frown and a furrowed brow at him.

"And . . . can I wire the hotel account five thousand dollars for her?"

"Yes, naturally."

"If I can use your fax machine, I can do it now before I leave."

"In the office," she said, leading him behind the desk and opening a highly polished wooden door.

"I have no business, Herr Leiden, but I must say it. I have known you many years. Forgive me if I go too far. You are a good man, sir, but I don't think Miss Jenny wants your money. She needs something else."

"I know that, Frau Holzman, how well I know that, but I don't think I'm the one to give her what she needs. I just can't."

"So," she said, shrugging her thick shoulders.

He sent his fax to his banker, giving his account number and that of the *Drei Könige*, and requesting that the wire transfer be made as soon as possible.

"I imagine the money will be in your account at least by tomorrow. I know that you will see that it gets to her."

"But of course."

"And if she needs assistance, transportation, plane tickets home, anything, please, you will look after her, won't you?"

"I am not the one who leaves, Herr Leiden."

"Right," he said, duely stung by her words and look. "I have to say goodbye to Jenny and the baby. Then I'll be on my way."

When he got back to the room, she had put on his yellow shirt, her yellow shirt now, and held the baby in her arms. "Just go. I couldn't stand a speech or a long goodbye."

"No speeches, Jen, but I have to tell you that the room is taken care of for as long as you care to stay." He took out his wallet and counted out one thousand of the twelve hundred D-Marks that he had. "This is emergency money, Jen, and I've

146

wired five thousand dollars to the hotel for you and Erika to get back home on."

"I don't want your money, Erik." Huge tears rolled down her cheeks, clearly visible in the room's half light.

"I know you don't, but you need it, so just take it. Don't let your feelings cloud your judgment, Jenny." He put the bills down on the foot of the bed.

"Just be like you, is that right?"

"Okay, if that's what it takes, yes, be like me, just this once. You and your baby have to get home. I've given you a way home, a start, Jenny. For God's sake, take it, for the baby if not for yourself. She deserves that, Jenny, doesn't she? It at least gives you a cushion." He took out a card from his wallet and a pen from his jacket pocket. "And here is a card with my shop telephone number, my fax number, and I'm writing my home phone on the back. You get home and you need anything, you call me. I mean *anything*, you understand?"

"You obviously can't give me what I need . . . what I want, Erik. I guess I'll just have to give up wanting and needing, won't I?"

"You've no idea how sorry I am, Jen, but I've got to go. I have to be in Los Angeles tomorrow. I told you that. If I complete this deal, everybody wins. Six stores instead of one, they have lots of cash and I have lots of expertise."

"Do me a favor, Erik . . . no, do yourself a favor. Before you sign that contract, or whatever it is, ask yourself when was the last time you were really happy. I know when that was, but maybe you've forgotten. Bigger isn't always better, and you know it."

"I want to kiss you Jenny, and the baby, but I don't know if you want to be kissed by me any longer."

"I'll always want you to kiss me. Always."

She held out one arm to him, the baby in her other. He bent and kissed her on the mouth, felt her parted lips and couldn't help but find her tongue, holding the kiss longer than he should have. Then he bent farther and kissed the baby on the forehead. She smelled wonderful, of powder and sleep, but most of all, of her mother. He had to pull himself away from her, away from them.

"See, I'm being good," she said, her bottom lip trembling as she chewed at the corner of her mouth, tears falling from her cheeks onto the yellow shirt.

"You were always good, Jen. Always were and always will be."

"Goodbye, Erik. You have your woodcarving? Mary?" she said with a start.

"I'll never go any place without her, Jen. Never. Now really, I have to go. I love you."

"Just not enough," he heard her say softly as he closed the door.

Epilogue

The three hours on the road had been a nightmare. The strange pain beneath his heart had gotten worse with every kilometer. And then the mad dash in the hope that he wouldn't be too late. The road wasn't too bad in most places, but in the shade, it was icy, the tires spinning, the car fishtailing unexpectedly, several times dangerously close to being out of control. He roared into the parking lot much too fast, slamming on the brakes, but catching a patch of ice beneath the tall fir tree, *the tree*, and then the bumper crashed through the split-rail barrier before the car came to a stop. He opened the door, jumped out, and without even bothering to close it, sprinted toward the entry way, bounded up the stairs, tore open the double doors with a great whooosh, and exploded into the warmth of the *Drei Könige*.

"Herr Leiden?" called Frau Holzman, an astonished look on her face. "*Was ist los?*"

"Nothing, Frau Holzman. I don't know if I was a fool for leaving or if I'm a fool for coming back, but I just couldn't do it . . . couldn't leave her."

"*Ach so!* Good that you have returned." Her face broke into a wide smile, her head nodding.

"She in the room?"

"But of course," she said, her hands clasped backward upon her breast.

He hurried down the hall, his heart hammering against his ribs, his blood roaring, and took the stairs two at a time, but as he approached the *Schwalbennest*, he realized that he no longer had the key to the room, her room now. He tried the handle, but it was locked. He knocked softly on the door. "Jen," he said, and knocked again, "It's me, Jen."

"Erik?" he heard her small cry from beyond the door. "Erik! Erik!"

"Yes, Jen." His heart felt as though it might burst. He could imagine what she must have been thinking and feeling all this time, the pain he had caused in these few hours, and he hated himself for it. Would she even open the door to him?

"Oh Erik! Erik!"

He could hear her moving on the other side, the baby crying now, and then the key turning in the lock, but the door handle still wouldn't turn, the door wouldn't open. "Jen, turn the lock."

"Ooh! Ooh! I can't . . . I can't get it open!" she cried, "Erik, oh, God . . . help me." The baby's crying grew louder, and she screamed above its crying, "Erik, oh God . . . oh, God . . . I can't . . . won't open!"

He could hear her jiggling the key, the tumblers turning over and over, backward and forward. "All the way around twice, Jenny," he said, his cheek pressed against the closed door, but apparently she didn't hear him.

"I can't . . . I can't . . . I can't," she chanted frantically, her small fist hammering against the other side, "Can't . . . can't . . . can't . . ."

"Two times around, Jen." He slapped the door with the flat of his hand to get her attention. "I'm here, Jenny, and I love you, two times around, honey," and then he heard the tumbler roll once more and the door latch give. She stood there holding the crying baby, frantic, lavender eyes red and puffy, thanks to him, but wide in surprise, his shirt, *her* shirt still damp from all the earlier tears that he had caused.

"Oh God . . . oh God! I thought you had . . . I thought you were . . . oh, God." Her eyes shone bright, welling once again, and she bit at her lower lip, chewed at the corner nervously.

"Are you . . . have you . . ." but she seemed unable to find the words she wanted, and with her free hand she reached up and touched his face, her fingers running over his cheek, his nose, his mouth, as if to make sure that he was real, not some figment of her longing.

The baby still cried, but it was a sound that now comforted him, a sound that now seemed full of hope and promise. He took her in his arms, them in his arms. "I tried to leave, Jen. Did, in fact, but it didn't work," he said, feeling her knees buckle, her body collapse against him. "Come on, Jen, let's get you back in bed."

As he helped her, he said, "I couldn't do it, Jenny. I tried to, but I couldn't. I just couldn't. Got halfway to the airport, but I had this pain, right here, as though my heart were being ripped out of my chest," he said, placing his hand on his breast, and then settling her into the bed, putting pillows behind her back, kissing her on the forehead, on the nose, on the mouth. "The further I went, the worse it got, Jen, and then I discovered that I was the one ripping it out, and I didn't have to do that. All I had to do was stop, turn around, and the pain would be gone, and the minute I pulled off the Autobahn and turned back toward you and the baby, it disappeared."

Her eyes glistened, and her breath came in short, ragged gasps. "Do you mean . . ." The tears streamed down her face. "Are you . . ."

"You've turned my world upside down, Jen. Everything that made sense a few days ago seems crazy now, and now every thing that seemed so crazy makes perfect sense. I don't know whether I should adopt you or marry you, Jenny. I only know that I can't conceive of a life without you in it, you and Erika."

"I don't want . . . to be . . . your daughter," she said between sobs.

"I don't want that either, Jen. It just got so complicated there for a while, for me, that is, trying to juggle everything, make everything right, keeping it all in the air without dropping any of it. I've only wanted what is best for you, Jenny, from the very beginning, but it seemed like the more I loved you, the harder that got. Hell, Jenny, don't you know that most of my life is behind me, while most of yours is still lies ahead of you?"

"And don't you know that I don't care about any of that? All I care about is you."

"I'm just afraid I'm being selfish, Jenny, taking so much from you with so little to offer, but I know I'll never be happy without you. All those years, Jen, all those years that separate us, they just seemed to stretch out into this vast canyon that I couldn't get across. You say it doesn't matter, but I worried that some day it might. Jenny, in ten years I'll be almost sixty, and in another ten, seventy."

"It doesn't matter, *mein Schatz*. It's your heart I love, that wonderful . . . gentle . . . generous . . . passionate . . . constant . . . strong . . . and loving heart. I know that's never going to change, ever. It will be my North, Erik . . . my polar star. All I'll have to do is look for it, and I'll never be lost again."

"Jenny, sweet Jen, my *Kleinod*, my little jewel, my small treasure."

"And your *Eiswein*, Erik? Am I your *Eiswein* too? I know I'm an oddity, I can't help that, but for you am I a rare and precious one?"

"Precious beyond words, Jen."

"I knew you loved me . . . knew it . . . but I thought maybe . . . maybe you didn't want the baby . . . but when I saw you with her last night, the way you were with her . . . I just couldn't understand it . . . any of it. I thought my heart would break, Erik, I really did."

"She was a big part of it, Jen, but not the way you mean. Do you know that when she's sixteen, I'll be sixty-five. I couldn't help but wonder how she would feel about a father that old? Would I be an embarrassment to her? Would my happiness someday make her unhappy? Would she wish that her mother had married someone else, someone younger? But you have to know that I love her, Jen, and not just because she's a part of you. I feel like she's ours, that that other guy was just some fluke, an accidental carrier. We brought her into this world, Jenny, you and I together. Isn't she more mine than his?"

"Oh, yes, yes, yes she is. You do love her, don't you? And me? You do love me?"

"I think I've loved you from that first evening, maybe even before, but when you came out of the bathroom wrapped in that towel, Jen, my heart leapt up into my throat, and I knew I was in trouble."

"A good trouble, yes?"

"Yes, Jenny, a very good trouble. While I was driving to the airport, I kept worrying about you and the baby. What if you needed a passport for the baby? What if someone tried to separate the two of you? I couldn't have borne that, Jenny. I would have gone crazy had I thought that someone had tried to take your baby from you, even for an instant. I worried that you might not be able to get a flight home. And then it dawned on me that I didn't even know where home was for you. I only knew that it wasn't with me, where it should have been, and I couldn't stand that."

"You're sure you want us, both of us?"

"More than I've ever wanted anything in my life, Jen."

"And your family, your children? What will they think? How will they feel?"

"Well, if they don't love you and Erika the way I do, screw 'em, Jen. Fuck 'em all. *You* are my family, and if the others don't want to be a part of us, they don't have to. We are more than enough, aren't we?"

"Oh yes, yes yes! Now I'm really going to cry, Erik. I prayed to the Virgin that you would come back. I didn't know who else to pray to, and I didn't know if she would even listen, but I thought she might because she's a mother too. I know I shouldn't have, that it was really selfish, but I did. I had to, Erik. I just couldn't lose you like that. I love you too much. I know I said I wanted her to watch over you, but what I really want is to watch over you myself."

"One of the Magi has come early, Jen," he said, on his knees beside the bed. "It took a blizzard and a snow of confusion for me to finally understand the wonderful gift that has been given to me."

"An early Epiphany?"

"Frau Holzman said that the *Drei Könige* was magical, didn't she?" He moved up onto the bed beside her, knowing that if they were ever separated again, it wouldn't be due to his failure of nerve. He kissed her, holding nothing back, greedy for her now, knowing that he could never get enough of her.

"I know you, Erik, how strong you are, that I'm the impatient one, but a month from now, I promise you, my love, an epiphany of another kind," she whispered into his ear, kissing it, her fingers stroking his hair. "My love . . . my love . . . my love . . ." she continued to whisper, lips moving against his ear.

He didn't doubt her words, but he also knew that he had never felt more satisfied. He didn't need more shops. He didn't need more money. He only needed her. Together they would watch the morning mists hang above the Rhein at Bacharach, the grape leaves turn on gentle slopes like maple and aspen in the autumn chill, even the Burgundian rise of Montrachet transmute to gold by the touch of an early morning sun. Together they would drink the new, unfiltered wine and feed on onion torte on a terrace high above the Mosel's horseshoe bend at Trittenheim. He knew now that this was all he wanted, all he needed, to feast upon her sweetness, to savor her essence for the rest of his life, knowing that of her he would never grow sated.

*